TO KILL &
KILL AGAIN

THIS IS A CARLTON BOOK

Original interviews and research material copyright ©
Brook Lapping 2001
All other text copyright © Carlton Books Limited 2001

This edition published by Carlton Books Limited 2001
20 Mortimer Street
London
W1T 3JW

A CIP catalogue record for this book is available from
the British Library.

ISBN 1 84222 204 X

Printed and bound in Great Britain

TO KILL & KILL AGAIN

How Britain's most famous serial killers were
identified, caught and convicted

MARTIN FIDO

CARLTON
BOOKS

CONTENTS

ACKNOWLEDGEMENTS

Grateful thanks, first, to Brook Lapping Productions for permission to use research material from their series "To Kill and Kill Again", and for reading my text to check against further material received by them and not known to me. And to Penny Simpson of Carlton Books and Carole Peters, Tina Darcy, Alex Raw and Sophie Milland of Brook Lapping for fielding my questions about it and, where possible, meeting my requests for more. Spelling of names normally follows that of the Brook Lapping researchers, as does dating of incidents where they established precise dates. Direct quotations from the following people are all taken from Brook Lapping interview material which may or may not have been broadcast: Kelvin Ashby, Suzanne Bennison, Clive Bouch, David Briffett, Martin Burlin, James Chadwin, Dave Cox, James Droney, Evelyn Dymond, Julie Evans, Ian Fairley, Ray Fisch, Chris Frayling, Mike Green, Fred Harrison, Roy Hazelwood, Rupert Heritage, Jane Hibbert, Pauline Hildreth, Dick Holland, Bill Hunt, Peter Jay, Winnie Johnstone, Danny Kilbride, Geoff Knupfer, Michael Massheder, Brian Masters, Caroline Owens, John Pollard,

Bernard Postles, Robert Ressler, John Rutherford, Elizabeth Scott, Ron Shaw, Harry Smelt, Bob Spiers, Ron Stocks, Alan West, Megan Winterburn, David Zackrisson.

Thanks to Mark Olshaker and John Douglas (and Messrs Scribner) for permission to quote from *Mindhunter*, *The Anatomy of Motive* and *The Cases That Haunt Us*. Thanks to Mike Berry for information about psychological profiling and profilers, and the Rosemary West trial. To Tom Witter and the team at Flame TV for access to detailed research on one serial killer, and to John Connor for insider views on police work. To Stewart Evans for confirmation of one piece of his unpublished research. To Paul Begg, Keith Skinner and all contributors to Ripperologist, Ripperana and Spryder's Internet Jack the Ripper message boards for keeping me au fait with enthusiasts' views on multiple murder and ongoing problems. To Richard Dawes for indefatigable copy-editing. To Paul Savory, without whose laptop in America and hospitality in London I should not have been able to complete this commission. To my agent, Richard Jeffs, who saw that I was free to write without administrative distractions. And to Karen, who has borne with my prolonged disappearance to the bookshelves and the keyboard at a difficult time.

INTRODUCTION

IS THERE ANYTHING NEW to say about Jack the Ripper, Haigh, Christie, the Moors Murderers, Dennis Nilsen or Fred West? Haven't these gruesome serial murderers been fully exposed in book after book?

Well, not quite as fully as you might think, was the discovery that television researchers made when they looked into the possibility of a television series on serial killers. There is ongoing newly published research on the historical cases that may not be familiar. There are witnesses and investigators whose stories have never been told. And there is the FBI's Behavioral Science Unit, throwing new light on every old case it examines and puts into context. And when the psychological context and the historical context are combined, the history of British serial murder offers a fascinating insight into the ways in which criminal detection has advanced, and the ways in which relations between police and press have often determined public attitudes.

The first notorious British serial murderer was "Sawney Bean", the Scottish cannibal who preyed on travellers along the coast of Galloway. He probably never existed, as no record of him is found anywhere until the seventeenth century, about three hundred years after his supposed execution. Likewise "Sweeney Todd, the Demon Barber of Fleet Street" was the completely fictitious creation of a Victorian blood-and-thunder writer, despite a recent undocumented book's pretence that he really existed. The first genuine killers to attract serious notice in Britain by the sheer incremental number of their crimes were Burke and Hare in 1828. Their motive for killing 16 people was purely commercial. They wanted bodies to sell to an anatomist. Their English imitators Bishop and Head (executed under the names Bishop and Williams) confessed to five killings, and thought that many other London "bodysnatchers" had attempted "burking". But they attracted far less public attention than the Edinburgh ghouls, whose crimes prompted one of the first experiments in forensic (which literally means court-related, not scientific) pathology as anatomists at Edinburgh University experimented on rabbits to establish the difference between bruising inflicted before and after death.

There were other nineteenth-century murderers who claimed more than 10 victims. Dr Palmer of Rugeley killed numerous creditors and relatives whose lives he had insured. Mary Ann Cotton disposed of unwanted husbands and children. These people attracted notice, but nobody thought of them as inherently different from any other kind of murderer. Like Burke or the mythical Bean and Todd, they acted from obviously rational and self-interested motives. It was the mysterious and undetected Jack the Ripper who first seemed to represent something strange and inexplicable.

Despite the even odder murders of Dr Cream, it was not until 1948, when John George Haigh claimed to have killed nine people in order to drink their blood, that attention again focused on the mystery of mass murderers' psychological motivation. Serious academic investigation of the problem appeared in 1979 when Dr R.P. Brittain published an article on "The Sadistic Murderer" and this was followed by Canadian anthropologist Elliott Leyton's suggestion that multiple murders perpetrated with no financial motive were an attempt by disadvantaged losers in rigidly stratified competitive industrial societies to take a bitter revenge on classes that excluded or threatened them. This explanation meshed, to some extent, with Colin Wilson's historically based suggestion that sexual serial killing (*Lustmörder* as the Germans had started to call it) had replaced murder for gain since industrialization had secured adequate food and shelter for the majority of people, and according to Maslovian psychology, the "self-realizing" need for physical comfort and security was now replaced by a need to establish an esteemed identity or some higher mental and spiritual gratification. Certain people whose inner belief in their own superiority was actually frustrated by personal inadequacy would then find horrible gratification in imposing themselves murderously on sexually desirable victims.

A very different and more mechanical approach to the supposed "epidemic" of serial murder in the late twentieth century was proposed by neuroscientist Joel Norris. In addition to certain psychological disorders, he suggested that a predisposition to serial killing might be caused by damage to the limbic area of the brain. This could be innate, or might be caused by head injury or the ingestion of excessive lead and cadmium which could occur in poor diet. Parallel genetic research was concurrently suggesting that the presence of an extra Y chromosome in men might be statistically related to an inability to control violent or lust-driven urges.

The fullest scientific basis for psychological assessment of such criminals came in the 1970s when Robert Ressler and John Douglas of the FBI Academy in Quantico, Virginia, began interviewing large numbers of convicted serial rapists and murderers across the USA and quantifying their results. From their work came the popular terms "serial murder" and "psychological profiling". The instruction they offered trainee detectives was intended to make a practical contribution to the difficult detection of "stranger" killers or rapists, and the work is continued by their successors in Quantico.

This was a highly sophisticated form of criminal detection. It aimed at prioritizing the direction of investigation rather than identifying a killer. Thus Douglas's correct observation that the killing of numerous black teenagers in Atlanta, Georgia, around 1980 was almost certainly the work of a young black male was intended to move the investigation away from the inaccurate public perception that this was some sort of racist or Ku Klux Klan-inspired sequence of crimes. The highly sophisticated conclusions the FBI has reached about the motivation for serial murder seems extraordinarily remote from the simple "lust" apparently proposed by the Germans in 1920. Yet, without it, the crimes of Dr Harold Shipman exposed in 1998 would be totally mystifying.

Detection has come a long way since 1888, when Chief Inspector John Littlechild, head of the Special Branch, remarked that observation and information were the chief tools of the detective. Surveillance of potential victims, suspected perpetrators and anticipated crime scenes remains an inevitable part of police work. The perennial debate over the use of disguise for surveillance has come to temporary rest with the general idea of minimal disguise. The perennial debate over the danger that informants with criminal associates may corrupt police officers rages on, with some officers now deliberately wiring themselves for all interviews to establish proof that they have neither countenanced criminality nor joined in criminal activity. But this has more bearing on drug dealing and related offences than on the "amateur" crime of sexual murder. The use of press relations to accelerate information from the general public has moved from the deliberate suppression of the idea when the Ripper murders were being investigated, to an intensely close cooperative venture in the investigation that ultimately led to Alun Kyte's conviction in 2000.

When Jack was carelessly leaving bodies on the streets of Whitechapel, nobody could take fingerprints from the comb and alleged coins he removed from Annie Chapman's pockets and left beside her body. Today the tiniest speck of his own blood spilled while he made his attacks could be sent for DNA testing and linked to him if he ever came into police hands. The history of British serial killers is a history of ever-improving police techniques, weaving through a switchback of constantly changing relations between police and public.

JACK THE RIPPER

THE WORKING DAY started early for Victorian artisans. At half past three on the morning of August 31, 1888 two carters were walking from their homes in Bethnal Green and east Whitechapel to their respective jobs in the City of London and Spitalfields Market, both a mile or so away. They didn't know each other. They were about five minutes apart. They were quite unknown to the public. Charles Cross and Robert Paul would have been astonished to learn that their names would be remembered a hundred years later.

What they found initiated the international interest in serial killers that now grips much of the world. Cross saw it first. Walking along Buck's Row, a narrow, cobbled street with warehouses on the north side facing a terrace of recently built cottages on the south, he spotted a bundle lying in the gateway of Brown's stable yard, between the western end of the cottage row and a huge, grim Board School: a monumental cube of sooty red brick with a crown of black railings to stop children from falling off its flat rooftop playground. Thinking the bundle might be a useful tarpaulin, Cross went over the road to take a look. He had found the body of a woman, lying with her skirts inelegantly pulled up above her knees. Before he could examine her closely, he heard Paul's footsteps approaching, and drew back into the shadowy gateway. Seeing that it was only another harmless pedestrian, he called him across, and the two looked closely at the still figure before them. Paul thought he could detect faint breathing. Cross thought the woman was dead, and decorously pulled her skirts down. But neither could miss a morning's work on her behalf. They hurried on westward up Hanbury Street, a long, curving road running for about half a mile from the western end of Buck's Row to the north-eastern corner of Spitalfields Market. In Hanbury Street they came across PC Jonas Mizen on his beat.

"You're wanted in Baker's Row," Cross told him, naming the street today known as Vallance Road, off which Buck's Row and Hanbury Street branched. After a few words of explanation, Mizen hurried away to the stable yard.

There was already a police presence at the scene. PC John Neil's beat brought him into Buck's Row, and flashing his bull's-eye lantern on the body he saw what the carters had missed in the darkness: the throat had been cut. He promptly signalled for help, waving and flashing his lantern toward the eastern end of the street, where he knew that his colleague PC John Thain would soon be passing along Brady Street, which formed a T-junction with the eastern end of Buck's Row. (The police were generally directed not to use their whistles during the night when householders were sleeping unless some emergency such as a fire required that they be aroused. The third Ripper murder seemed such an emergency, given the state of public panic, that police whistles were heard from a quarter of a mile away at 1.00 a.m., summoning aid to the body.) When Thain arrived, Neil said to him, "For God's sake, Jack, fetch a doctor," and Thain hurried away, collecting his cape from Barber's knacker's yard in parallel Winthrop Street, where, earlier on his beat, he had left it with the night-working slaughtermen.

Mizen arrived from the other direction, and Neil sent him to fetch a hand-ambulance – a wheeled stretcher with straps and a canopy, generally used for conveying drunks or obstreperous arrestees. Mizen headed back toward the Whitechapel Workhouse Infirmary in Old Montague Street, and, before further police reinforcements could arrive, Neil was joined by two slaughtermen from Barber's.

They were soon supported by Dr Llewellyn, a general practitioner from Whitechapel Road, just three hundred yards away, whom Thain had awoken. The nearest doctor to hand, he was not a specialist pathologist. His opinion, like that of every other doctor in the case, carries none of the scientific weight that modern forensic pathology brings to post-mortems. The police divisional surgeons who carried out most post-mortems and had more experience than anyone else in ascribing the causes of unexplained deaths were appointed in the first place to provide medical attention for officers taken ill or injured in the course of their duties. Forensic pathology was a secondary skill, acquired by practice. In 1888 William Henry Willcox, pioneer of the academic study of the science, was just 18; Bernard Spilsbury, who made it world-famous, was ten.

Dr Llewellyn's examination was cursory. He pronounced the unknown woman dead and directed that her body be taken to the mortuary at Whitechapel Workhouse Infirmary: a crude shed whose inconvenience and proximity to the windows of the infirmary ward was dangerous, insanitary and the subject of much acrimonious complaint by the divisional police surgeon, Dr George Bagster Phillips.

A third slaughterman soon appeared, followed by a nightwatchman called Mulshaw who had been guarding sewage workings in Winthrop Street and had been told by an unidentified passer-by,

"Watchman, old man, I believe somebody is murdered down the street." All these civilians hung around the scene for as long as there was anything interesting to see.

Two adjacent divisions of the Metropolitan Police were instantly involved in the case. The body had been found in J Division (Bethnal Green). But Mizen belonged to H Division (Whitechapel). And from H Division he directed Sergeant Kerby to Buck's Row. Kerby brought another constable with him and became temporarily the senior officer on the scene. He told Mizen and Thain to take the body to the mortuary as Llewellyn required. When it was lifted, the policemen noticed that the woman's clothing was soaked with blood down the back, leaving only a tiny crimson pool in the gutter under her neck. Llewellyn later estimated the quantity as about a wine glass and a half.

Inspector Spratling of J Division was in Hackney Road when he heard the news and hurried to take command at the scene of crime. He followed the body to the infirmary, and started making notes on its appearance as he waited for pauper attendants to come and open the mortuary shed. He was probably the first to observe the deep, jagged cut running down the woman's abdomen: the first of the infamous "rips". Dr Llewellyn had to be summoned again to make a more thorough examination.

As Spratling left the mortuary to return to Buck's Row, Detective Sergeant Enright was left in charge of the body. When he, too, departed, he gave strict instructions that it was not to be touched until Dr Llewellyn had examined it. The pauper attendants, Robert Mann and James Hatfield, disregarded this order, stripped the body, washed it and laid it out on the mortuary table to await the doctor. So it was probably their ministrations rather than the victim's personal hygiene that cause Llewellyn to comment on her surprisingly clean thighs. And they may have required careful washing because of the three or four additional fierce slashes on her lower abdomen.

Llewellyn also observed bruising on the face and neck which he felt might have been caused by the killer steadying the woman's chin with his right hand while he cut her throat from left to right. This, coupled with his view that the other knife cuts might all have been made from left to right across the body led him to postulate that the killer was left-handed or ambidextrous: an opinion which stayed in Ripper lore for many years. In 1972 Donald Rumbelow's masterly *The Complete Jack the Ripper* – still the best introduction for a novice in "Ripperology" – put forward the suggestion that the prostitute victims might have turned their backs on the murderer, offering him standing intercourse from a posterior position, which allowed him to grab them round the neck with his left arm and slash the throat from left to right with his right. This interpretation convinced pathologist Dr Bill Eckert, founder of the Milton Helpern Institute of Forensic Sciences, when he heard it on one of the guided Ripper walks Donald Rumbelow has conducted for the past 10 or 12 years.

Inspector Spratling was as hygienic as the two mortuary attendants. Back in Buck's Row he oversaw some cleaning up of the scene as a boy from the end cottage sluiced a bucket of water over the traces of blood in the gutter. Then the police fanned out to make fruitless house-to-house enquiries up and down the road, and to learn that running footsteps had been heard in Brady Street in the small hours, sounding like a man chasing a woman. There were also a few drops of blood in Brady Street. These led to the erroneous speculation that the woman might have been killed some distance from the place where she was found. In fact Dr Llewellyn and all who saw the body in Buck's Row had no doubt that she lay exactly where she had been murdered.

The body was now the responsibility of the coroner. The first widely reported serial murders suffered a degree of coroner-related publicity that would be impossible today. Victorian coroners were often competitive, touchy and vociferous. Doctors felt that all coroners should be medical men. Lawyers felt they should all have the legal training to conduct a proper inquest with some respect for the rules of evidence. The post was elective, and a particularly ferocious and dirty partisan campaign had been fought in 1887 for the East London division, which included Whitechapel. Mr Wynne Baxter, a flamboyant and dressy lawyer running in the Conservative and Unionist interest, had defeated Dr Roderick MacDonald, a highlander and Radical believer in Home Rule for Ireland. Shortly afterward the division was split in two, and, somewhat irrationally, Tory Baxter was made coroner of Whitechapel and the docklands, where left-wing working-class and Irish voters predominated, while Radical Dr MacDonald presided over Baxter's home turf: the more respectable and conservative boroughs of Hackney and Stoke Newington, running down into Shoreditch. As it happened, the body had been found in a gateway under Dr MacDonald's jurisdiction, and then moved to the mortuary under Mr Baxter's. In law, the inquest was to be held where the body "lay", and at this point nobody contested Baxter's right to hold the hearing on it. Later, some politically motivated squabbling when the Ripper's last victim "lay" under Dr MacDonald's jurisdiction led twentieth-century purveyors of sensational theories to propound the notion that Baxter was nobly trying to expose a police conspiracy to shield VIPs and Freemasons implicated in the murders, while Dr MacDonald was the tool of an establishment cover-up. The truth was that Baxter, himself an ardent Freemason, seized the chance of some self-aggrandizing publicity by holding long and disputatious inquests criticizing the police, while Dr MacDonald acted with almost precipitous expedition to get the obvious fact of "murder by a person or persons unknown" confirmed, and clear the matter out of his court and the headlines as fast as possible.

The first duty of coroner and police was to establish who the woman was. Like all the Ripper's victims she moved in illiterate circles and carried no papers or writing which might have identified her. Like many of them, she wore a large quantity of filthy, ragged clothing, including several skirts and underskirts, as the poor streetwalkers of the East End often had no fixed place of residence and had to carry all their possessions with them as they shifted from one cheap common lodging house to another. Her dress was described in the newspapers, but although the buttons on an old ulster she wore had what seemed the distinctive moulded pattern of a groom holding a horse, nobody recognized her. A laundry mark stencilled on one of her petticoats showed that it came from Lambeth Workhouse. (This victim would prove to have a history of pilfering linen and clothing from places where she lived or worked.) The workhouse matron was summoned, but failed to identify the woman.

It would be another 12 years before fingerprinting came to Scotland Yard, and some time after that before it was realized that corpses could have their fingerprints taken, allowing them to be identified if their prints were on file or identifiable on property in their homes. Photography of corpses in mortuaries had not reached the skilled level at which a touched-up resemblance of living features could be created for publication. Identification depended on finding someone who could recognize the body.

Nobody around Buck's Row knew the woman. Nobody in the street had heard anything. Nobody was especially surprised that streetwalkers used the dark gateway into the stable yard for standing fornication, leaning against the wall. Nobody was excessively surprised that a lady of the night had been murdered. The incident might have passed with minimal public comment had it not been for the second such knifing of a Whitechapel streetwalker in three weeks. The inquest on Martha Tabram, found with 39 stab wounds on the landing of a tenement building a quarter of a mile to the west of Buck's Row, had just concluded with the unsatisfactory verdict of "murder by a person or persons unknown". It had received unhysterical and factual newspaper coverage. But it meant that the Buck's Row incident was immediately presented to the public as "Another Woman Murdered in Whitechapel". The foundation was laid for a running story.

Eventually a young woman who had been with the Buck's Row victim in Lambeth Workhouse identified her as Mary Ann, or "Polly", Nichols, and this was confirmed when her estranged husband came and identified her lugubriously, saying that, seeing her "like this", he "forgave her" for what she had done to him. In fact there was some dispute over the reasons for the marital rift. Nichols maintained that his wife had been intolerably drunken and left him to start a liaison with another man. But her family thought that he had caused the break-up by having an affair with the nurse at one of Polly's confinements, in consequence of which his eldest son had been removed into his grandparents' care.

Such soap-opera drama would have been grist to the mills of a later generation of sensational newspapers. But in 1888 the Press was still learning the art of maximizing profits by colouring the news with petty scandal and sickly sentiment. Mrs Nichols's family history was described in its proper place, at the inquest, without the embellishment of lachrymose interviews with her children or parents. Her professional history as a dishonest maidservant, an estranged housewife and mother and then a vagrant, living the previous year among the unemployed camped in Trafalgar Square, was not reported by every paper.

But that connection with the unemployed lent the death a useful interest to the Radical evening papers: the *Star* and the *Pall Mall Gazette*. The economy was in recession, and every weekend a large gathering of the unemployed marched to Trafalgar Square for a protest rally. They were under heavy police protection – or, rather, the property of the good burghers along their route was protected by the body of constables drafted for extra duty to police the rallies. Throughout the summer of 1887 Trafalgar Square had been the site of a mass encampment of homeless unemployed, where rival socialist groups attempted to drum up support and fan revolutionary feeling, requiring a presence of two thousand policemen to keep them from one another's throats. In October the Metropolitan Police Commissioner, Sir Charles Warren, persuaded the Home Office to let him prohibit all public meetings in the square. On "Bloody Sunday" (November 13), a vast mob converged on the square from north and south London to challenge his authority, and spend the afternoon fighting with police and soldiers. Many of the demonstrators and police were hospitalized. It was widely reported that one or more of the unemployed had died from their injuries (though this has never been conclusively confirmed). And Warren, a liberal intellectual "model of a modern major-general", appointed by Gladstone's government before it fell for espousing Irish Home Rule, was excoriated as a traitor in the left-wing press. The weekly demonstrations in the Square had to be tolerated.

So when it seemed that a sequence of unsolved murders was taking place in the East End, it was easy to accuse the unpopular Warren and his force of wasting public money in harrying peaceful demonstrations by men without work (and, for good measure, spying improperly on Irish Nationalists in an attempt to tar them all with the brush of terrorism), when he ought to be catching the monstrous assassin. Furthermore, it was all happening in the East End, where the Radicals rightly expected that their candidate, Annie Besant, publicist of the successful matchgirls' strike, would win the local seat on the newly formed London County Council. A series of outrages against destitute East End streetwalkers gave a heaven-sent opportunity for journalism exposing the poverty tolerated in the district by Conservative and mainstream Liberal politicians alike. The *Star* and the *Pall Mall Gazette* seized the opportunity, and were astonished by the enormous sales that resulted from their featuring gruesome murder reports. The respectable press was compelled to follow suit or lose readership. Even the High Tory *Morning Post* could not afford to despise the subject or eschew the criticism of the police that became an inevitable part of the story.

The police themselves accidentally gave a lead to this reporting. It had got back to the London newspapers that J Division detectives believed the murders of Polly Nichols and Martha Tabram were by the same hand, as was that of Emma Elizabeth Smith in April of that year. So there was a sequence of three to report.

That last claim was actually wrong. Emma Smith had been attacked and subjected to a brutal indecent assault with a stick or pointed instrument which led to her death from peritonitis. But her assailants were three thieving youths, not one sexually perverted murderer. She said so before she died in hospital a few days later.

Here we have in embryo the basis for later treatment of mysterious and serial killing. The police tell the papers of a bloody murder and a mystery. The papers tell the public. The public is voracious for more sensational information. The newspapers start examining police methods with a critical eye. And the widespread castigation forces some tactical reforms.

The Metropolitan Police acted to meet criticism about the precipitate cleansing of the murder site. New standing orders laid down that a constable discovering a dead or incapacitated person in a public place should remain with the body until a police station had been informed and a senior officer took charge. Like many reactions to sudden public protest, this swift closure of the stable door overlooked the fact that the horse had not escaped at the time in question. PC Neil had not left the scene of crime until Sergeant Kerby took over. And the new standing order gave another constable serious concern three years later when the last murder tentatively ascribed by the British Press to the Ripper took place. On February 13, 1891 PC Ernest Thompson found 26-year-old streetwalker Frances Coles lying in a dark alley under a railway arch near the Royal Mint with her throat cut. She was still alive, and he remained with her until she died and assistance arrived. But as he found the body, Thompson heard footsteps "proceeding in the opposite direction towards Mansell Street", and until his own untimely death at the hands of a knife-wielding troublemaker in 1900, he feared that he had missed the opportunity to chase and capture Jack the Ripper.

Still, if the standing order was not perfect in every case, it represented a move in the right direction. Present-day Scenes of Crime Officer Ron Stock has said, "The key to good forensic evidence is early preservation of a scene: something that nowadays is driven into young recruits." Today yellow-and-black scene tape saying, "Police. Do Not Cross" is promptly posted to hold the public back from trampling on possible evidence. The presence of three slaughtermen and a nightwatchman to keep the police company and gawp at the initial investigation would not be tolerated. There might be little hope of finding scientific evidence in the meagre pool of blood left at Buck's Row, but nobody would recklessly slosh water around that might carry away any small thing the murderer had dropped.

In October 1888 Dr Robert Anderson, Assistant Commissioner in charge of the CID, commented on the killer's miraculous good fortune in committing a sequence of murders over a period of weeks without leaving a single clue. Since the police examined suspects by the score, and were, in the words of Inspector Frederick Abberline, "lost in theories", he evidently didn't mean that they hadn't a clue where to start looking. Rather he used the word pedantically, meaning that the murderer had not left a physical clue like a trouser button or a footprint to narrow down the direction of their search among the intangible suggestions provided by informants and theorists. Later Dr Anderson complained that a clay pipe found at the last murder site had been casually thrown away when it might have been "a clue".

Inspector Abberline's presence in the case marked police recognition of another potential detective problem: divided jurisdictional authority. With H and J Divisions each having their own Criminal Investigation Departments under their own Local Inspectors, there might have been friction had Inspector Reid of H wished to carry out a different form of investigation from Inspector Helson of J. And so Abberline, who was one of the elite group of senior CID officers stationed at the Commissioner's Office in Scotland Yard, was sent to take charge of enquiries. He was the fittest man for the job, having previously served in H Division for 14 years, rising to be its Local Inspector for nine of them. He probably had a better knowledge of the East End and its criminals than any other officer in the Metropolitan Police. On occasion he confirmed to the newspapers that he was "in charge of the case", and in many respects he was equivalent to the Senior Investigating Officer who would be appointed in a similar case today. But in hierarchical terms he was not the ultimate head of the team. In the absence of Robert Anderson, on sick leave on the Continent, a memorandum personally endorsed and probably drafted by the Commissioner himself appointed Inspector Donald Swanson to take command of the case, with instructions that he was to be "the Commissioner's eyes and ears", and all important evidence was to be sent to him at Scotland Yard. When Anderson returned a month later, the Commissioner and the Home Secretary placed him personally in charge, and he spent two and a half days studying the accumulated reports and witness statements. Such hands-on detective work by such a senior officer would be unthinkable today, even if it amounted to no more than visiting the crime scenes and examining all the paperwork. But many of the late-Victorian police top brass, drawn from the educated and officer classes – unlike the ordinary artisan policemen, who could usually only rise to the rank of superintendent – rather enjoyed mucking in and playing detective.

Neither Anderson nor Abberline had any quarrel with the actions taken by H and J Divisions. Spratling and Helson immediately deputed officers to take statements from surrounding householders: these came up with little useful information. Subsequently, as more murders built up the importance of the investigation, Scotland Yard organized an immense house-to-house search with interviews covering much of Whitechapel, most of Spitalfields and parts of St George's-in-the-East, and the police were impressed by the public cooperation with this invasion of privacy. But it still produced no important evidence that we know of. Inspector Henry Moore, who took over from Abberline when the feeling of crisis diminished, had many regular informants from the fringes of criminality, and he turned to them for advice. They could not help.

At the same time street patrols were increased with drafts from other divisions until the area was swamped with beat officers and the prostitutes complained that they could not earn their living without some copper clumping into the shadows where they were trying to service their clients. Plain-clothes officers worked the area in simple disguises: wearing a frock coat and gaiters and carrying a whip to look like a coachman, for example, or donning a coalman's fustian trousers tied at the knees, sacking apron and distinctive cap. One even dressed as a woman, but this received no official approval. There was a moment of embarrassment in north London (for panic and anxiety spread far beyond the affected East End), when a beat policeman saw an obvious man in woman's clothing, thought he might be a CID colleague in disguise and asked, "Are you one of us?" The transvestite was in fact a journalist hoping to catch the Ripper off his guard. Thinking the bobby had made a homosexual pass at him he hit out, and was arrested for assaulting a policeman.

In the end observation, like information, proved ineffective in solving the case. Later experience would prove that it requires a hefty dollop of good luck to make standard observation a vital element in serial "stranger" murders.

When the local plain-clothes detectives started asking for information from prostitutes on the streets, however, a suspect emerged. Several women claimed to have been threatened by a sinister Jewish immigrant whom they referred to as "Leather Apron", since he often or always wore one. Descriptions of him in the newspapers seem to have been imaginatively highlighted to make sensational stories. We cannot say for sure whether he really was aged about 40, had a strikingly short neck, hung around the Princess Alice pub on the corner of Commercial Street and Wentworth Street watching the street-walkers, had a friend called "Mickeldy Joe" and used a cudgel, knife or even pistol to threaten the women. We can be sure that he existed and had been seen in Crossingham's Lodging House in Dorset Street wearing a two-peaked cap (like a deerstalker without earflaps), since Timothy Donovan the deputy (or manager) confirmed that he had seen him there and kicked him out for threatening a woman. Detective Sergeants Enright and Thick seem to have played a major role in collecting this information, and it would appear that it was Thick who suggested that Leather Apron might be a local boot finisher named John Pizer.

By the time Pizer had been traced to his home in Mulberry Street and arrested by Thick, a second murder had taken place and fear of Leather Apron had risen to hysteria since a wet leather apron was found near the body. It proved to be the innocent property of one of the residents in the house where the body was found, but the public was outraged by the idea of a Jewish artisan going around killing women and there seemed a serious danger of anti-Semitic rioting. The police were relieved to put Pizer up at the second victim's inquest, asserting that he really was the prostitutes' Leather

Apron (which may be doubted, since he and his neighbours subsequently denied it, and he had been unemployed for two years, with his leather apron left at home) and that he was not the murderer (which is certain: he had been talking to a policeman in another part of London at the very time when Polly Nichols was being killed). Despite Abberline's great knowledge of the Whitechapel underworld, that was the only really useful general information to be elicited. He oversaw the arrests of a number of men described as behaving suspiciously. Several were found to be insane and sent to asylums. Some were convicted of lesser crimes. None was the murderer. Abberline's own forays on to the streets at night were most notable for his humane practice of carrying sixpences to give to late-working prostitutes, so that they could get a bed in the safety of a common lodging house instead of risking their lives on a predatory murderer's patch.

Several prostitutes continued to tell the newspapers that they suspected a specific man who threatened them on the streets, but whose name they did not know. One newspaper believed that Sergeants Thick, Enright and Godley continued to look for the man suspected by the prostitutes a good three weeks after Pizer's arrest and clearance had supposedly ended the hunt for Leather Apron.

But by that time three more victims had followed Polly Nichols, and the murderer had acquired the nickname that would relegate Leather Apron to the memories of crime historians. Annie Chapman, second of the "canonical five" who many of the police at the time believed to have died at the same hand, was killed around half past five in the morning of September 8. It was already daylight at that time of year, and a woman called Mrs Durrell (or Long – police files noted that she was known by both names) saw her with a man whose age she estimated at over 40 and whom she took for a foreigner, standing outside the street door of 29 Hanbury Street. The man was saying, "Will you...?", to which Annie replied, "Yes".

The door opened on to a narrow passage stretching the depth of the house next to the stairs and the adjacent shop which occupied the ground floor. A back door opened on to two steps which led down into a narrow yard with a privy for the use of all tenants. Prostitutes often made use of the corridor and yard, conveniently screened from the street and always accessible as the doors were left open all night for the house's many occupants. A few moments after Mrs Durrell's sighting, young Albert Cadoche went out to the privy of the house next door. He heard a woman's voice from the yard of number 29 say a quiet "No", and, shortly after, the thump of something falling against the tall wooden fence. He thought nothing of it.

Twenty minutes to half an hour later one of the occupants of number 29 got up and went out to the yard. There, lying between the steps and the fence on his left, he saw Annie Chapman's body. Her skirt had been pulled up, her abdomen ripped open and the intestines severed and thrown over her shoulder.

Annie's was the first Ripper body given a post-mortem by H Division's police surgeon, Dr George Bagster Phillips, who ultimately examined more of the bodies in the case than anyone else, and came to some firm opinions. He clashed with coroner Wynne Baxter at the inquest as he tried to withhold any description of the posthumous injuries he had found, maintaining pedantically that he was required to ascertain the cause of death: not detail atrocities committed subsequently. Baxter insisted on hearing them, though he cleared the court of women and boys. And so it was learned that Annie Chapman's uterus and ovaries, with about two-thirds of her bladder, had been cut out and taken away. Phillips was the first and firmest medical witness to suggest that the mutilations indicated medical or anatomical skill. Indeed, he claimed that the crude hysterectomy would have taken him half an hour under perfect conditions, whereas this murderer had completed the job in a confined space during five minutes of dawn light.

Already Baxter had criticized the police for their slipshod handling of the crime scene in Buck's Row. Now he and Phillips joined forces to deplore the inadequate and insanitary mortuary provided for the post-mortem. Phillips had observed a very neat arrangement of Annie's comb and a piece of muslin cloth at her feet, which apparently the police had overlooked. Two brass rings she had been wearing the previous evening were missing, and Phillips saw bruising on her fingers where they had been pulled off. A press canard alleged that these rings, together with two copper coins, had formed a ritualistic pile at the victim's feet. This erroneous belief lay behind a good deal of misplaced ingenuity in later years as theorists attempted to ascribe the murders to Freemasons or psychologically compulsive ritualists.

Baxter trumpeted another erroneous theory, claiming that an American doctor was offering substantial sums of money for specimens of the womb, to be sent to subscribers to a monograph he was writing. Ever since Burke and Hare murdered 16 people and sold their bodies to the anatomist Dr Knox in Edinburgh in 1828, there had been public anxiety about the ethical standards of xperimental doctors. The *British Medical Journal* was quick to refute Baxter's scare. They knew of the doctor in question. He had left England over a year earlier. He had paid nothing for the wombs he needed, but received them *gratis* from hospital mortuaries, as his intent was serious research, not a silly, grisly complimentary gift to subscribers. Baxter dropped his claim silently, and it would be of no lasting importance were it not for the extraordinary fact that Inspector Abberline believed it, never learned of its refutation and used it in support of a very dubious theory he came out with in 1903.

Baxter was also responsible for the inquest on the third "canonical" victim, Elizabeth ("Long Liz") Stride. (The nickname "Long" attached itself automatically to Londoners called Stride as "Chalky" attached to the name White, "Dusty" to Miller, or "Nobby" to Clark(e).) She was a Swedish immigrant married to and separated from an Englishman, and, although in her forties, a handsome woman, unlike her predecessors. Her identity was not immediately established, however, as for no apparent reason a Mrs Mary Malcolm presented herself at the inquest declaring that she identified the body as that of her sister, Mrs Elizabeth Stokes. When Mrs Stokes herself came forward to disprove the claim, Mrs Malcolm discreetly disappeared. The little imbroglio exemplified the problems of victim identification in the days before reliable photography, fingerprinting and other scientific aids to policing.

Elizabeth Stride's murder is significant on two counts. Several witnesses described a man or men she was with on the night of September 29–30, one of whom may well have been her murderer. This seems particularly possible as one witness, a recent Jewish immigrant called Schwartz with hardly any English, actually saw her attacked in the street by a young drunk who hurled an anti-Semitic insult at him as he ran away from the scene. A neighbour's sighting that was definitely not of the murderer a few minutes before the body was found led to the long-standing belief that the Ripper carried a little black bag to hold his knife. In fact the owner of the bag was identified: an innocent salesman carrying home samples of empty cigarette boxes.

The body was found in the yard of a socialist immigrants' club by the club steward, who drove up in a horse and cart. She had just been killed, and it has generally been assumed that the noise of the cart coming down Berner Street (now Henriques Street) led the killer to hide or take flight. Whether he was actually Jack the Ripper is the second important question raised by this murder. Although Elizabeth Stride's throat had been cut, her abdomen had not been mutilated. The knife used appeared to be different from that employed in the second and definite Ripper murder to take place that night. (Measuring the depth and breadth of knife wounds, and noting whether the weapons were sharpened to a point and sharpened on one or both edges, was a forensic pathological skill practised at post-mortems in 1888.) If the young drunk seen attacking her five or ten minutes before she was found really was her killer, then his conduct in shouting aggressively to scare off a male passer-by was remarkably unlike what we now expect of serial murderers.

On the other hand, for what precise reasons we don't know, the press in 1888 were absolutely convinced that Elizabeth Stride was a Ripper victim: the first on "the Night of the Double Murder". It was believed that the killer had been interrupted by the approaching cart and left with his blood-lust unsatiated. This led him to walk about three-quarters of a mile and find another prostitute, whom he attacked with unprecedented frenzy. Roy Hazelwood of the FBI's Behavioral Science Unit finds this conclusion realistic and persuasive. "I do believe that the person who killed Elizabeth Stride also killed the second victim that same night," he says. "Again, very close proximity, within a short period of time, following an interrupted attack, and the mutilation was more horrendous than anything that had taken place up to that time. So I think by his being unable to act out his fantasies – his abhorrent fantasies – with Elizabeth Stride, that just added to his anger and his stress, so that when he finally got a victim that night, she suffered the consequences of it."

In addition, the second victim that night was also seen with her killer, and the witness, a respectable Jewish gentleman called Lawende, gave a description not unlike that given by Schwartz: a youngish man, aged perhaps about 30, with a light moustache, wearing a cap and a pea-jacket. This, again, is similar to the description, given by yet another witness, of a man seen in a street parallel to that where Stride had just been killed. And the location fits the route of a man travelling from the first to the second murder site of that night.

The second murder was under the jurisdiction of a completely different police force: the City of London Police, who were and are responsible to the Lord Mayor, not the Home Secretary, and who police the square mile of the ancient City of London, right in the middle of the Metropolitan Police region. The involvement of a second force entailed difficulties which could not easily be overcome from above as Scotland Yard had done with H and J Divisions by giving Abberline command over officers working on the ground. Although the Home Secretary ordered complete cooperation and there were regular meetings between City and Metropolitan senior officers, the Home Office wearily noted that long reports from the City Police seemed to withhold more information than they imparted. The Commissioner of the City Police offered a reward for information. Sir Charles Warren wanted to do likewise, but was prohibited by Home Office guidelines laid down when it was found that rewards encouraged hoaxers. Scotland Yard was concerned that the early release of the information that they suspected a local Jew had provoked anti-Semitic tension. Metropolitan officers were therefore forbidden to talk to the press. The City Police, by contrast, were encouraged to chat to journalists, and were generally praised for being forthright and dedicated, while the Met's "Defective Force" was unfairly ridiculed by *Punch* as bumbling and inept.

The body in the City was found by a beat policeman in a dark corner of Mitre Square, close to the two great historic synagogues abutting on Whitechapel which had encouraged so many Jewish refugees from Bismarck's nationalist laws and Russia's pogroms to settle in that parish. The woman lay on her back, horribly exposed with her skirts drawn up. In addition to the deeply cut throat and savage rip through the abdomen there had been a great deal of cutting and slashing inside the body which had severed her intestines and extracted her uterus and left kidney, both of which had apparently been taken as trophies. In addition her face had been attacked. A savage lateral cut ran through her upper lip to the gum, nearly severed the tip of her nose and sliced off the edge of an ear lobe. In an odd ritual gesture, inverted "V"s pointing up toward her eyes had been carved on her cheeks, and her eyelids had been nicked.

The City detectives, like Spratling's men at Buck's Row, immediately fanned out across the neighbourhood enquiring whether benighted passers-by had seen anything. They had better luck than the Met at the first murder. In a doorway on Metropolitan territory in Goulston Street, about eight minutes' walk away in the direction of Whitechapel and Buck's Row, an extra duty Metropolitan beat constable found a piece of the victim's apron thrown into a dark doorway. It had been cut off in the square and used to wipe the perpetrator's hands and possibly knife. On the wall above it was a chalked message which would become a bone of contention. It read: "The Juwes [or "Jewes"] are the men that will not [or "not the men that will"] be blamed for nothing." The uncertainty about the exact wording and misspelling resulted from City and Metropolitan Police transcribing it differently. The graffito was on Metropolitan territory, and although the acting City Police Commissioner, Major Henry Smith, was very anxious that it should be preserved until daylight and photographed, Sir Charles Warren followed the advice of H Division's chief, Superintendent Arnold, who wanted the writing washed off before market traders arrived and interpreted it as evidence that "a Jew" had killed again. For this he was severely criticized. Inspector Moore believed the writing to be the murderer's work. Assistant Commissioner Anderson also thought it was reckless destruction of evidence, even though a preponderance of police detectives knew that the area was full of hoax chalk markings purporting to be the work of the murderer, and few believed this had any connection with the case.

The apron, on the other hand, was an incontrovertible clue, showing that the killer had proceeded north-east out of the square in the direction of the Whitechapel and Spitalfields border, and possibly the portion of Commercial Street known to the local vicar as "the wicked quarter mile" since it harboured so many prostitutes and the filthy common lodging houses which accommodated them.

The City Police did one other thing that exceeded Metropolitan detective activity. They took a wide range of mortuary photographs of the victim, including close-ups of her face to show the precise cuts, and pictures of her naked body pegged upright against the wall to expose the extent of the abdominal injuries (heavily stitched after the post-mortem, and looking worse than they had originally because of the pathologist's long incision along the length of the breastbone). Frederick William Foster, an architect and surveyor from the City, sketched the position of the body in the square, and sketched and labelled the various injuries as the face and body were examined in the mortuary. Ever since these sketches were discovered among the London Hospital archives in the 1960s and published by pathologist Francis Camps, and the photographs were traced and published by the former City policeman and historian Donald Rumbelow in the 1970s, we have had a clearer image of the Mitre Square murder than any of the Ripper's other outrages, though the Met, perhaps stimulated by the City, took two scene-of-crime pictures of the final atrocity.

But for all their efforts, the City were as confounded as the Met in their attempts to identify the killer. They established that the Mitre Square victim was a chirpy little soul called Catherine Eddowes, who had actually been in City Police custody for being drunk and disorderly (singing, dancing and allegedly imitating a fire engine) on the pavement of Aldgate a few hours before she was killed. But as the City Police had the humane practice of releasing drunks from the cells when they had sobered up, rather than having them clog the courts for their trivial offences, she was released after midnight, and had the misfortune to meet Jack the Ripper.

Within a day he was known by that name. It came from a letter and a postcard received by the Central News Agency the previous week, and forwarded by them to Scotland Yard. The letter, dated September 25, 1888, and written with red ink in a neat copperplate hand, read:

Dear Boss

I keep on hearing the police have caught me but they wont fix me just yet. I have laughed when they look so clever and talk about being on the right track. That joke about Leather Apron gave me real fits. I am down on whores and I shant quit ripping them till I do get buckled. Grand work the last job was. I gave the lady no time to squeal. How can they catch me now. I love my work and want to start again. You will soon hear of me with my funny little games. I saved some of the proper <u>red</u> stuff in a ginger beer bottle over the last job to write with but it went thick like glue and I cant use it. Red ink is fit enough I hope <u>ha</u>. <u>ha</u>. The next job I do I shall clip the ladys ears off and send to the police officers just for jolly wouldnt you. Keep this letter back till I do a bit more work, then give it out straight. My knife's so nice and sharp I want to get to work right away if I get a chance. Good luck.

Yours truly

Jack the Ripper

Dont mind me giving the trade name

wasnt good enough to post this before I got all the red ink off my hands curse it No luck yet. they say I'm a doctor now <u>ha</u> <u>ha</u>

The postcard, written immediately the news of the double murder appeared in the papers, read:

> I was not codding dear old Boss when I gave you the tip, youll hear about saucy Jackys work tomorrow double event this time number one squealed a bit couldnt finish straight off. had not time to get ears for police thanks for keeping last letter back till I got to work again.
> Jack the Ripper

In Assistant Commissioner Anderson's absence – he was not rushed home from his allotted three months' sick leave until the "double event" occurred – these missives were taken to be the genuine work of the murderer. The nick in Catherine Eddowes's ear lobe, and the fact that Elizabeth Stride had suffered the common accident of having a pierced ear ripped or grown out into a small slit, were misinterpreted as evidence that the killer had indeed made abortive attempt to cut off an ear for the police. Anderson had no doubt the letters were the work of "an enterprising journalist". They were mailed in the Fleet Street newspapers' postal district of London EC and not Whitechapel, London E. They were perfectly spelled though imperfectly punctuated. They were sent by somebody who knew that news agencies gave the widest distribution to information they received. The first letter, if made public, would keep up interest in a story which seemed to be waning as there had been no murder for nearly three weeks and the inquests were over.

Roy Hazelwood of the FBI confirms that the most expert of today's police would concur with Anderson's opinion that the famous letters were not a clue. "Serial killers do carry out correspondence with the media; correspondence with the police; correspondence with television journalists," he has said. "However, Jack the Ripper was a paranoid schizophrenic in our opinion. If you read those letters they're very, very well thought out. They've been planned and probably practised before they were sent in."

But the letters received wide publicity, and for the best part of a hundred years the world believed that the Whitechapel murderer had devised his own dreadful name. Donald Rumbelow rightly observed that the name itself goes far in explaining his continuing fascination.

The case raged in the newspapers throughout October. The police received hundreds of unsolicited letters offering more or less useless advice. They were encouraged to try bloodhounds, and experimented with a pair, ultimately finding that they were of little use on well-walked city pavements. A well-known busybody asylum keeper with legal training pushed himself into the news. He said that asylum attendants could catch the Ripper better than any policemen because their trained eyes could spot a lunatic at large. He claimed to have learned who the Ripper was and acquired his bloodstained boots. The police interviewed him and found that he was exaggerating to boost his own importance, and the "blood" on the boots was mud. A correspondent accused General Sir Sam Browne of the murders. There were two generals of that name on the army lists at the time, one of them the inventor of the cross-over belt. Dutifully the police trudged over to Sir Sam's home in Kensington and had him confirm what they never doubted: he could not possibly be the Ripper. The Queen followed a newspaper suggestion that the movements of cattle boats should be checked, since the vaguely regular occurrence of murders toward the ends of weeks suggested some loose schedule. An obsessive nuisance went even further, printing out lists of schedules and accusing named Portuguese seamen, changing his suggested "perpetrator" each time the police laboriously demonstrated the innocence of the latest. The police checked all the butchers and slaughtermen in the City and East End, and established positively that no shochet, or Jewish ritual butcher, could be the killer, since shochets' knives were curved and the Ripper's was straight.

For many years writers on the Ripper followed the press attacks and accused the police of confusion and incompetence. While it is true that they were unable to agree unanimously on the most likely suspect, and practically all their arrestees that we know of proved their innocence and were discharged, this does not in itself point to incompetence. Stewart Evans, editor of all the Metropolitan Police and Home Office files on the case, and himself a former policeman, has concluded that even by today's standard the police did a pretty good and thorough job in 1888. Of course they lacked today's forensic scientific tools. But supposing they had found a fingerprint, or a blood sample which proved to be different from the victims', or had taken a semen swab? The labs would still have required a suspect in custody to provide fingerprints or samples for comparison. And Stewart's calculation is that there is not much more that could have been done today to trace such a suspect.

October and the first week of November passed with no further murder. And then, on November 9, the Lord Mayor's Show was interrupted by newsboys crying that the Ripper had struck again.

It was true. In the worst atrocity yet, in a tiny room off Dorset Street, the most dangerous thoroughfare in "the wicked quarter mile", the Ripper had gone with the first of his victims to have a rented room of her own in which to turn tricks, instead of standing up against walls in dark corners. And with the security of an indoor appointment and all the time he needed, the Ripper had effectively cut the unfortunate Mary Jane Kelly apart. Her throat was cut. She was disembowelled and her abdominal cavity emptied. He had cut up through the diaphragm to extract her heart, which he took away (as Dr Bond ambiguously noted and his assistant, Dr Hebbert, more clearly confirmed in a supplementary report). He had cut off her breasts. Her face had been slashed and stripped of flesh; her ears cut off. Her right thigh was stripped of flesh to the bone. There was blood all over the floor; pieces of flesh and organs scattered over the bed and on the table. There were not, however, organs and pieces of carrion hanging from nails or picture hooks on the walls. That was a newspaper embellishment that became part of the legend.

The newspapers' search for more details on this youngest and best-looking of the victims set up a number of additional false trails which can mislead researchers today, though they don't seem to have hampered the police at the time. There were suggestions that Mary Jane Kelly had a child being cared for in some other part of London; and suggestions that she might have been out visiting her child when witnesses found by the police placed her picking up clients off the streets of Aldgate and Spitalfields. All this, coupled with the fact that a couple of witnesses thought they had seen her alive on the streets on the same morning her body was found and pronounced to have been dead since the small hours, has invited armchair speculation that the unrecognizably mutilated body was not really that of Mary Jane Kelly, but that she escaped and some dark conspiracy placed another person on her bed. Nonsense like this didn't hold up the police for a moment. They consigned Mrs Caroline Maxwell, with her belief that she spoke to a hung-over Mary Jane Kelly around eight o'clock in the morning, to the limbo of misremembered misinformation. But it is worth bearing in mind that estimating a corpse's time of death is still a tricky and relatively imprecise process, and that Dr Bagster Phillips had certainly placed Annie Chapman's death several hours too early, misled by the body's rapid cooling in the chill dawn air.

The post-mortem on Mary Jane Kelly was carried out by Dr Phillips in the presence of the City's Dr Brown and Dr Thomas Bond, police surgeon to A Division. It is evident that Assistant Commissioner Anderson trusted Bond more than Phillips, and that the two doctors agreed on very little. Bond was given the task of writing a report surveying all the medical evidence in all the cases, and he came to one radically different conclusion from Phillips. Bond thought all five "canonical" murders were by the same hand, and the murderer "had no scientific nor anatomical knowledge ... not even the technical knowledge of a butcher or horse slaughterer". Phillips thought the murderer showed definite skill in the cases of Chapman, Stride and Kelly, and was probably the source for coroner Baxter's confident and implausible assertion that Eddowes was killed by "an unskilled imitator".

Rather interestingly, Bond drew his medical conclusions together in the form of a primitive deductive offender profile, which can be compared with a modern one drawn up by the best and most experienced offender profilers in the world today. He wrote:

> The murderer must have been a man of physical strength and of great coolness and daring. There is no evidence that he had an accomplice. He must in my opinion be a man subject to periodical attacks of Homicidal and erotic mania. The character of the mutilations indicate that the man may be in a condition, sexually, that may be called satyriasis. It is of course possible that the Homicidal impulse may have developed from a revengeful or brooding condition of the mind, or that Religious Mania may have been the original disease, but I do not think either hypothesis is likely. The murderer in external appearance is quite likely to be a quiet inoffensive looking man probably middle-aged and neatly and respectably dressed. I think he must be in the habit of wearing a cloak or overcoat or he could hardly have escaped notice in the streets if the blood on his hands or clothes were visible.
>
> Assuming the murderer to be such a person as I have just described he would probably be solitary or eccentric in

his habits, also he is most likely to be a man without regular occupation, but with some small income or pension. He is possibly living among respectable people who have some knowledge of his character and habits and who may have grounds for suspicion that he is not quite right in his mind at times. Such persons would probably be unwilling to communicate suspicions to the Police for fear of trouble or notoriety, whereas if there were a prospect of reward it might overcome their scruples.

How does this profile strike a modern-day profiler? "I think that the fact that a ... medical doctor hypothesized that he might be wearing a coat and a cloak ... would be an early form of profiling. But that goes to the physical appearance," Roy Hazelwood of the FBI comments. "We go more to the personality and characteristics and traits. I believe that the physician gave as his justification that he could then move through the community with blood on his clothes. Well, anyone could move through that community with blood on their clothes because there were knife fights, there were murders constantly, there were rapes in that neighbourhood. Having blood on you would certainly not attract attention to you." Roy Hazelwood knew all about profiling Jack the Ripper. In 1988 Dr Bill Eckert, founder and principal of the Milton Helpern Institute of Forensic Sciences, was asked by Cosgrove Muerer Television to suggest an interesting case for them to kick off a series of new solutions to unsolved mysteries. Knowing the success the FBI was having with the new technique of profiling, Dr Eckert suggested that the Behavioral Science Unit be asked to formulate a profile of the Ripper. To that end, all the leading crime historians, "Ripperologists" and theorists who had written on the case were interviewed, and the substance of their historical accounts of the case reviewed by Ripper historian Paul Begg. The approved data were passed to John Douglas, the head of the Unit. Douglas, whose down-to-earth experienced police officer's approach meshes comfortably with the academically trained intelligence that earned him a Doctorate of Education, invited the equally respected agent Roy Hazelwood to join him, and the two created the FBI profile of Jack the Ripper. Never before had such a wide range of accurate information from all the serious historical experts been assembled.

Douglas listed the key points on which a profile could be based:

1. No evidence of sexual assault.
2. Subject killed victims swiftly.
3. Subject was able to maintain control of victims during the initial blitz-style attack.
4. Subject removed body organs from some of the victims, indicating some anatomical knowledge or curiosity.
5. There is no evidence of physical torture prior to death.
6. There is severe post-mortem mutilation.
7. There is evidence of manual strangulation.
8. In most cases blood was concentrated in small areas.
9. Rings were taken from one of the victims.
10. The last victim was killed indoors and was the most mutilated. Subject spent considerable time at the scene.
11. Time of death in all cases was in the early morning hours.

The profilers noted that the crimes were committed within easy walking distance of each other. The killer's initial "comfort zone", where he felt familiar with his surroundings, was in the vicinity of Whitechapel underground station, some way to the east of "the wicked quarter mile" where he probably shifted his activities as increased police observation alarmed him. He lived and worked in Whitechapel, either his home or his workplace being close to Buck's Row. He would have committed previous violent crimes or arson in that area, though they had never been connected with the murders.

Since four of the bodies were discovered within minutes of the killing, and all but the last crime took place on open streets where people might be expected to be about, the murderer fell into Robert Ressler's category of the "disorganized serial killer": a man with limited education, intelligence and foresight, who struck opportunistically as the craving and opportunity came together, without planning a means of safe escape. He selected prostitutes as his victims because they were easily available, and just possibly because he had contracted a venereal disease from one and wanted generalized revenge. He would not be acting from demented religious or moralistic convictions. As a disorganized killer, the murderer was highly unlikely to set up a conscious challenge to authority, so he would not be the author of the Jack the Ripper letters.

He could be safely predicated as a white male. There are no known cases of lesbian serial lust-murderers of women. And except where a prostitute population includes different races, the lust-murdering serial killer usually strikes women of his own colour.

He would look normal, giving the streetwalkers no reason to suspect anything unusual about him. Acquaintances would think of him as a quiet, shy loner: withdrawn, obedient and reasonably orderly in his appearance. He would drink in local pubs before each murder, and return to some safe place where he could clean himself up afterwards. He had definite paranoid tendencies, possibly exacerbated by some defect like a stammer or a malformation which led to his being mocked in childhood. His paranoia encouraged him to carry knives about with him. And his insanity increased as the murders progressed, since the later ones were more frenzied and disorganized than the earlier.

Roy Hazelwood's recollections 12 years after the profile was drawn up stressed that the killer came from the lower echelons of society: he was certainly not, as some theorists had proposed, a doctor or lawyer or member of the royal family. He was single and had never married, with an intense – indeed, lunatic – fear and hatred of women. His bizarre conduct would probably have brought him to police attention, though in the context of late-Victorian Whitechapel it need not have led to his being suspected of murder

A plethora of new suspects would probably make it impossibly expensive to repeat such an exercise today. The five suspects presented to Douglas and Hazelwood were Queen Victoria's grandson, Prince Albert Victor; a self-styled black magician calling himself Dr Roslyn D'Onston; the royal family's physician, Sir William Gull; a young barrister and schoolmaster called Montague John Druitt; and the obscure immigrant lunatic Aaron Kosminski. Only the last two were taken seriously by rigorous historians at the time, as they were identified police suspects named in memoranda drafted by Anderson's successor, Melville Macnaghten. (He also identified a Russian confidence trickster called Michael Ostrog, but his historical career had not at that time been discovered and made public.) Prince Albert Victor, Sir William Gull and D'Onston all emerged from dubious sources and latter-day armchair detection. Since then another important police suspect has been discovered: the American quack doctor Francis Tumblety, and some commentators have suggested that Elizabeth Stride's and Mary Jane Kelly's steady boyfriends, Michael Kidney and Joe Barnett, who also came under police scrutiny, should be held responsible for their murders at least. One academic historian has leaned toward Abberline's 1903 suggestion that the bigamist murderer George Chapman was the Ripper. And John Douglas's attention having been drawn to information about another obscure Jewish lunatic, he has concluded that he "or some one very like him" was more probably the Ripper than Kosminski.

But if the suspects who merited contemporary police investigation have held the attention of most of the more rigorous Ripper historians, other theories have been given a wide public airing and attracted more notice. The painter Walter Sickert, the poet Francis Thompson, Oscar Wilde's friend Frank Miles, a man called William Bury who murdered his wife, and Prince Albert Victor's Cambridge mentor J.K. Stephen have all found adherents. A forged diary purporting to be the work of Inspector Abberline turned up alleging that Winston Churchill's father, Randolph, directed a conspiracy of Freemasons to commit the murders. Another diary, whose dubious provenance has stimulated fierce ongoing debate as to its validity or the date of its forgery, purported to be the work of Liverpool cotton broker James Maybrick, detailing the ways in which he carried out the murders. Since Maybrick's wife was convicted of poisoning him the following year, this sensational story has attracted enormous attention, and Maybrick probably holds the field as the best-known candidate for Jack the Ripper at present. He has been accorded the vote of an academic who surveyed the field for an article in *History Today:* perhaps the first appearance of Ripper studies in a journal with no commitment to crime history.

But for most people the mystery remains gloriously mysterious. Stewart Evans, who has read everything there is to read on the subject, discovered Tumblety and studied the official files more closely than anyone else, is convinced that it will never be solved. Donald Rumbelow, an MA in history as well as an accredited London guide and former police officer, has memorably remarked that, on the Day of Judgement, when Jack the Ripper is called, all of us who have studied the case will look at the unknown figure that steps forward and ask, "Who...?"

And that question mark forms in everyone's mind whenever an undiscovered serial killer is seen to be at large in a great city. So the uncaught maniacs are given sobriquets recalling the great original: the uncaught "Jack the Stripper" in 1960s London; Peter Sutcliffe the "Yorkshire Ripper" in 1970s Leeds and Bradford; "Jack the

Snipper", cutting dresses to expose buttocks in London in 1977. And his title has been gruesomely translated into language after language: *l'éventreur* in France; *il squartatore* in Italy; *der Bauchauchschlitzer* in Germany.

1888–1949

THE POLICE IN 1888 could not have anticipated that within four years another suspect would pop up: the second serial killer in post-industrial England. The Scottish Canadian Dr Thomas Neill Cream poisoned five prostitutes from Lambeth, where he had studied at St Thomas's Hospital. Cream, unlike Jack the Ripper, was a supremely organized killer. He gave his victims drinks or capsules containing strychnine, and did not stay around to watch their agonizing deaths a few hours later. He would almost certainly never have been caught had not his wish to profit from his murders by blackmailing prominent people tangled insanely with his characteristic serial killer's narcissistic wish to enjoy his anonymous appearance in the limelight. He wrote dotty letters accusing public figures of having murdered the women in Lambeth: Earl Russell, the royal physician Sir William Broadbent and the heir to W.H. Smith's book-selling empire, Fred Smith MP. He exposed himself as the real killer by evincing knowledge of some of these deaths before they were made public or, in one case, even suspected of being anything other than death by natural causes. And he finally made sure he was caught by sending a blackmailing letter to the father of one of his fellow lodgers in Lambeth, so that investigation of the boarding house revealed the presence of a cross-eyed, heavily moustached doctor, as described by a street-smart prostitute who had covertly thrown away the pill he gave her.

Cream's modus operandi was quite unlike the Ripper's. His motive (quite apart from the half-hearted blackmail schemes) was less directly sexual than the Whitechapel murderer's, and much closer to a relatively pure form of that desire to control and manipulate to the ultimate degree which would surface again a century later in Dr Harold Shipman. But he was the serial killer of a number of London prostitutes, which inevitably aroused some suspicion. And this was strengthened by the report that hangman Billington heard him say, "I am Jack the —" as the drop fell on the scaffold.

Whatever Cream may have said, he wasn't. Donald Rumbelow established categorically that he was in Joliet prison, near Chicago, throughout the Ripper scare, serving a life sentence for an earlier insurance scam which had turned on his poisoning a patient's husband. It was the world's misfortune that his family's influence and mistaken belief that he had recovered from his undoubted madness led to his early release and return to England in 1891.

Twelve years later England saw another serial killer go to the gallows, and once again it was suggested that he was the Ripper. This time, none other than Inspector Abberline voiced the suspicion. George Chapman, born Severin Klosowski in Poland, was a humble barber-surgeon. He came to England in 1888 and worked in the East End. He began the habit of contracting bigamous marriages, and after a period in America from 1891 to 1895, formed three unsatisfactory relationships which he terminated with poison. In 1897 he killed Isabella Spink, with whom he had been living since

1895. He became a publican and seduced his barmaid, Bessie Taylor, in 1898, poisoning her in 1901. And he seduced and poisoned her successor, Maud Marsh, in little over a year. This time the girl's parents and doctor were suspicious. A death certificate was refused, and Chapman went to the gallows in 1903.

And Inspector Abberline said to Inspector Godley, "I see you've got Jack the Ripper at last." In long interviews with the *Pall Mall Gazette* he tried to dispose of the obvious objections. The modus operandi was different? Well, said Abberline, a man morally capable of poisoning three women between 1897 and 1902 was morally capable of knifing five others nine years earlier. (The evasion of the point at issue was worthy of a politician under pressure.) There was a remarkable gap of time between the murders of Mary Jane Kelly and Isabella Spink? Abberline believed there had been Ripperesque killings in New York while Chapman was there. (There had actually been one very doubtfully similar murder of an old bag woman in New Jersey.) The Ripper was a sex maniac whereas Chapman murdered from rational, if evil, motives? No, Abberline believed the Ripper was rationally motivated, too, collecting wombs for Mr Wynne Baxter's long-exploded American doctor. It is remarkable that one of the only two academic historians to examine the case in detail has reached the indecisive conclusion that although Chapman isn't likely to have been the Ripper, Abberline is more likely to have been right than anyone else proposing a suspect. (The other academic, a social and literary historian specializing in the Victorian period, concurs with John Douglas and Bill Eckert.)

In 1912 an apparently natural accident was actually the beginning of Britain's next serial killer's career. Like Chapman, George Joseph Smith murdered three bigamously espoused "wives". His famous method, "finding" them drowned with the soap in their hands, earned him the nickname "Brides-in-the-Bath".

Smith was caught in 1915 because his clever MO was sufficiently poignant to win sympathetic little notices in the press. Relatives and associates of his first two drowned "wives", as well as Sir Arthur Conan Doyle, creator of Sherlock Holmes, noticed the oddity of yet another husband having the unusual misfortune of finding that his new wife had passed out and drowned in the bath while he was supposedly out buying groceries. They sent the incriminating cuttings to the police, and when Smith was found to have insured his "wives'" lives, he was destined for the gallows.

But even more than Chapman, he was rationally motivated. Murder was only the last and wickedest way in which he tricked, entrapped and exploited marriage-hungry spinsters. He had used them as thieves, planted on the domestic staffs of wealthy people. He had "married", robbed and deserted lonely women with some property. Finally he insured and drowned those who were less well off.

Proving that their deaths were no accident was a matter of forensic pathology. It should have been easy. Bernard Spilsbury was now semi-officially the "Home Office pathologist". He had made his name in the Crippen case, identifying a mark on a flap of skin as an operation scar which showed it to be the last remains of Mrs Crippen. He would be able to find signs if Smith had concussed or forcefully drowned his victims. And had he drugged them, Professor Willcocks was improving laboratory expertise all the time, refining the Marsh test for the presence of arsenic to quantify the amount; establishing how it might make its way into soaked hair without having been ingested.

Spilsbury has today something of a reputation as the great prosecuting witness, who swayed juries unfairly and won convictions that were not always justified. His testimony, however, was always governed by what he had seen and not what he thought the prosecution wanted him to say. And he came close to saving Smith from the gallows when he could not work out how Margaret Lofty, the last victim, had been held under water. She was too tall to have slipped under the contents of the short tub. Yet there wasn't a mark on her body, as there must have been had Smith forced her under. A nurse in a bathing costume was put experimentally in the filled tub, and Spilsbury and Detective Inspector Arthur Neil tried unsuccessfully to hold her down without leaving a bruise or a graze on her. It was Neil who had the bright idea of pulling her ankles up in the air. The nurse's head slipped straight under the water, and she did not move. It was a good thing that Spilsbury was present. It took half an hour's work with artificial respiration and smelling salts to revive her. When the nurse could speak again, she reported that slipping into and under the water backwards had sent a rush of water into her mouth and nostrils which caused her to black out immediately.

Smith had the great Edward Marshall Hall as his counsel. But his case was doomed when prosecutor Sir Richard Muir won the argument to allow all three drownings to be described. Common law insists that a defendant is tried for one crime and one crime only. Except under peculiar special conditions (like making an issue of prosecuting witnesses' bad character), previous offences may not be put before the jury.

There was a precedent, however, in the case of Dr Cream. His modus operandi was so cautious that it would have been impossible to prove conclusively from any one case alone that a prostitute who died after an appointment with him had done so because he gave her strychnine. It required the cumulative evidence of dying women who said they'd been given a pill or a drink by a cross-eyed punter, together with identification testimony from one who had discreetly thrown away the capsules he gave her. Cream's counsel protested that this was trying him for seven murders and not one. The judge, Sir Henry "Hanging" Hawkins, let the evidence go forward as proof of "pattern". And Richard Muir put the same argument to the court trying Smith, which, in a more elegant decision than Hawkins's, agreed. Rex v. Smith is today the determining case cited by lawyers to justify introducing evidence of similar crimes "to prove pattern".

But was Smith a serial killer at all? There was no element of "lust murder": indeed, the necessary marital sex his conjugal confidence tricks entailed was said to disgust him. There was no evidence that he took pleasure in killing a bride. Smith was unhealthily evil, but it may be doubted whether he was in any real sense mad. He certainly did not fit the mental pattern ascribed by veteran FBI psychological profiler Robert Ressler to Jack the Ripper: "an individual who started off some sort of a borderline mentally ill person and then slipped through the five homicides deeply into psychosis".

But Ressler does not limit the title "serial killer" to the Victorian doctor's "satyriast" or the Victorian Police Commissioner's "sex maniac". He is aware that "Serial homicide ... as it's perceived by the public is ... motivated by lust and mental disorder ... and delusions, hallucination and things of that nature." But he comments, "That's not always accurate. There are those that commit a series of homicides based on greed, and motivation of gaining money, gaining items of value. Improving their own life at the expense of others and they would be lumped into a category that I would refer to as the criminal competition area."

Roy Hazelwood and John Douglas use almost identical words in defining serial killing: words that inevitably admit Smith to the company. "A serial killer," says Douglas, "is someone who has murdered on at least three occasions, with what we call an emotional cooling-off period between each incident. This cooling-off period can be days, weeks, months, even years. Occasionally it is only hours. But the important consideration is that each event is emotionally distinct and separate." And Hazelwood, considering Smith's successor John George Haigh, the "Acid Bath Murderer", says,

"Haigh was a serial killer because he killed three or more victims over a period of time, with an emotional cooling-off period between the crimes. Whether or not it was for greed; whether or not it was to prevent his identity from being made known to the police; or whether or not it was sexual ... he is still a serial killer."

Both Hazelwood and Douglas differentiate between the serial killer and the spree killer, whom Douglas describes as "someone who murders at two or more separate locations with no emotional cooling-off period between the homicides. Therefore, the killings tend to take place in a shorter period of time, though, of course, if the serial killer's cooling-off period is short enough, he might even work faster than the spree killer."

This distinction might almost be pointed directly at a question posed by the only English multiple murderer to emerge between Smith and Haigh. "The Black-Out Ripper", Gordon Frederick Cummins, as Colin Wilson has remarked, is less well known than he might be, because he murdered in wartime when newsprint was rationed, and so his crimes were never fully reported. But he was horrifyingly impressive. Between February 9 and March 14, 1943 he killed four women and attacked two others. Three of his victims were savagely mutilated. His last mutilating murder was followed, not preceded, by his two unsuccessful assaults. That frenzied evening of March 14, comprising three murderous assaults in three separate locations, suggests the spree killer rather than the serialist with his cooling-off period. But the spree killer usually proceeds on the run, travelling from one crime to the next, stopping only to sleep and eat, often in the home of his next terrorized victim. Carl Starkweather and Caril Fugate, who killed 10 people in a week's rampage through Nebraska and Wyoming in 1951, are the classic example. Typical spree killers run until they are caught, or killed.

Cummins, however, went quietly back to his RAF camp after his three assaults and tried to behave as though nothing had happened.

Was this because the authority of the armed forces was even stronger than his lust to continue his spree? Or was he a serial killer with the shortest of cooling-off periods?

Twenty-five years old and married, Aircraftsman 525987 was preparing to start pilot training. Cummins was not popular with his fellow aircraftsmen: he was too distant, superior and, they sensed, phoney. He pretended to be of noble descent: the illegitimate son of a lord. They nicknamed him "the Duke", with no admiring intent. He thought himself superior to his situation and underrated by the world. Thus far we have the egocentric and narcissistic psyche of the serial killer.

On February 9 he strangled Miss Margaret Hamilton, a former schoolteacher doing war work as a chemist. Her body was found in an air-raid shelter in Montagu Square, not far from Marylebone Station. The motive was apparently theft to sustain the "aristocratic" front Cummins tried to keep up. Miss Hamilton's handbag had been ransacked. Cummins's fingerprints were found and examined by Detective Superintendent Fred Cherrill, the brilliant head of the Fingerprint Bureau who devised a means of marking a magnifying glass with measured concentric rings and using its measurements as a basis for filing and retrieving individual prints. Cummins had no criminal record, so Cherrill had nothing with which to compare the dabs. But his knowledge of the position taken by the hand during the strangulation led him to predict that the killer would prove to be left-handed.

This was the first time fingerprinting played any part in an English serial-murder case, and Cherrill's prediction was proved absolutely accurate when the next victim was found two days later. The tin-opener used to "rip" former stripper turned prostitute Evelyn Oatley lay near her body, and with a thumb and fingerprint, Cherrill could confirm that this killer was left-handed.

Cummins had never been an "organized" killer. He had left

fingerprints at two of the murder sites, and was caught after the reckless act of grabbing a woman on the open street, albeit in the black-out. His intended victim screamed and broke the strap of his gas-mask holder. Cummins ran away and made no attempt to recover the gas mask, though his service number stencilled on the case must inevitably lead to him.

He was instantly traced. His fingerprints led to his being charged with the murder of Mrs Oatley. And his stupid defence of complete denial, offering no explanation for the evidence against him, led the jury to convict him after a mere half-hour's deliberation. He certainly evinced the kind of rising frenzy and accelerating disorganization that Roy Hazelwood perceived in the Ripper. And his courtroom appearance might well have given rise to the classic utterance, "You couldn't say he made a fool of himself. God had already done that for him."

It might have, but it didn't. For that was said of another murderer that year: Harry Dobkin, who likewise pleaded ignorance and denial in the teeth of the evidence. Dobkin was not a serial killer. He was a fire-watcher who killed his estranged wife in 1941 and buried her in a church porch opposite his post, before starting a small fire there and reporting it as enemy action. When the porch was cleared the following year and the body was found, it might easily have been taken for a bomb victim. But a young pathologist was starting to vie for the mantle of Spilsbury. Keith Simpson of Guy's Hospital noted that the skeletalized body had been cut up before going under the floor of the church porch. So the victim had been murdered, not killed by bombing. He also found the upper jaw complete. Tracing Dobkin's wife's dentist confirmed that this body was hers, and from that date to this dental records have played a vital part in establishing murder victims' identities in some of the most sensational serial cases.

As they did in the Haigh case in 1949.

JOHN GEORGE HAIGH

J OHN GEORGE HAIGH is not invariably considered in the context of
serial killing. He was tried for only one murder: that of Mrs Olive
Durand-Deacon. His sensational mode of disposing of her body
and his equally sensational claim to have been motivated by a
compulsion to drink blood have led to his legendary status as the
"Acid Bath Murderer" or "Vampire Killer". This has obscured the
equally sensational fact that he utterly obliterated two families
before murdering Mrs Durand-Deacon, and explains why Roy
Hazelwood found it necessary to assert carefully that Haigh was
indeed a serial killer.

Haigh was born in Stamford in 1909 and brought up in
Yorkshire. His parents were devout Plymouth Brethren and, despite
later attempts to paint them as rigid puritans who warped their son,
a good and loving father and mother. Of course the Brethren led
odd lives by twentieth-century standards. Alcohol, tobacco, gam-
bling, the theatre and reading novels were all prohibited as godless.
But many an evangelical Church of England clergyman would have

abstained from all five at the end of the nineteenth century, when Haigh's parents were born. What made and makes Plymouth Brethren different is their view of themselves as a "peculiar people" who put their godliness at risk by socializing with "gentiles" not of their persuasion. Yet in this respect the Haigh family were far less cranky than many of their co-religionists. They encouraged their son's musical talent – he became a first-rate amateur pianist – and when he won a scholarship to train as a chorister at Wakefield Cathedral they allowed him to take it up and go on to become the cathedral's assistant organist. It seems a shame that these very decent people, who bore with criticism from their co-religionists for thus risking John's perpetual commitment to the Brethren, should later have been misrepresented by his defenders as narrow-minded bigots who did him permanent damage. Despite the extreme contrast between the High Church ritual of Haigh's schooling and the religious austerity of his home, this was by no stretch of the imagination a dysfunctional family. Haigh was sufficiently intelligent and adaptable to reach his own beliefs and personality between the two environments. All his life he would enjoy theological discussions, keeping his end up by his intimate knowledge of the Bible. And his parents, while emotionally broken when their son's appalling wickedness was revealed, never withdrew their love from him, just as they had always refused to cut themselves off from him earlier when he proved a common criminal and served three prison sentences.

Perhaps Haigh's great charm owed something to this admirable couple. Many people who knew him found him fascinating, rewarding, delightful company. Hard-nosed policemen and prison officers, men who would happily have seen every murderer swing, nonetheless admitted that Haigh was "the nicest murderer they ever met" – of all the ironic titles.

His appearance was reassuring. He had striking blue-green eyes and a perpetual friendly half-smile. He was neat and clean: "dapper" was the word often used of him. His hair was carefully parted and Brylcreemed; his little moustache trimmed closely back to his lip. He favoured three-piece suits, often in brown shades. He wore well-cut overcoats and lemon gloves. And he washed his hands repeatedly: pretty certainly a psychological sign of guilt and insecurity.

He had reason to feel guilt. From the time he was 24 he made most of his money by crime. After leaving school he had a succession of short-lived jobs. He was an apprentice engineer with a car-sales firm; a local government clerical officer; an insurance salesman. He picked up useful skills from these experiences. He learned the ins and outs of the car market and became a competent mechanical engineer. He came to understand the general workings of finance, and particularly the ways in which it could be forwarded by business correspondence. He perfected a very beautiful script and turned his calligraphic skills to imitating other people's handwriting and signatures. For fun at first. But ultimately as a notable forger.

None of these jobs was making him rich quick. And Haigh had discovered that the world of fast cars and pretty women had more appeal than the religious worlds of either the cathedral or the Brethren. His music and his knowledge of the Bible were all that really survived from his upbringing. He loved Beethoven, Chopin, Tchaikovsky (except for the *1812 Overture*) and, especially, Mozart. But he also loved the Alfa-Romeo which he bought when he branched out on his own as an entrepreneur. He brokered insurance policies. He bought and sold cars. He described himself as an engineer and "inventor" to Betty Hamer, the pretty daughter of a music-hall comedian, whom he met and married when he was 24 and she was 21. He described himself as a company director on the marriage certificate. He was so wrapped up in himself that he did not notice when Betty and her sister, bored by a classical concert he took them to, left before it was over. Betty agonized over whether she was doing the right thing in marrying John. When her sister said he was rich, she replied anxiously that she didn't know where his money came from.

Four months after the quick and almost clandestine register-office wedding in Bridlington, to which no relatives came, she found out. Haigh was arrested and charged with fraud. He had been approaching garages which he knew to be undergoing financial difficulties. He pretended to have customers who wanted to buy cars. With access to legitimate garages' letterheads, he produced a quantity of forged applications for hire-purchase agreements, and finance companies happily sent him back funds through the garages he purported to represent. How he intended to stave off the need for some repayment is not clear. He was caught and sentenced to 15 months in Wakefield Prison.

He wrote moving letters of apology to his parents, promising to redeem the past on his release. Betty, who was pregnant, handed her baby over for adoption as soon as it was born. There was no divorce, but the couple separated absolutely. And from that moment Haigh's sex drive started to dwindle. His sexual inclinations, unlike those of most other serial killers, were perfectly normal. But his libido became extremely low. (There may be an interesting comparison with George Joseph Smith's alleged distaste for sexual intercourse.)

In 1935 Haigh came out of prison. The Brethren had formally excommunicated him as soon as he was convicted. His grieving parents welcomed the sinner back into their home in Leeds, and saw him set up as assistant manager of a dry-cleaning shop. Haigh was able and ambitious. He increased the firm's business substantially, and seemed to be making his way back up the ladder. Then the owner was killed in a motor accident, and his widow closed the business. Haigh was unemployed and almost friendless. He made the fateful decision to go to London.

It was still more fateful for Mr and Mrs Donald McSwan and their son William. Donald McSwan was a local government officer with the London County Council. Nearing retirement, he had saved his money and invested in pinball arcades. Young William, just Haigh's age, managed these for his parents, and as the business expanded he needed help. When he advertised for a "secretary/chauffeur", he was delighted that the respondent, John George Haigh, also had engineering skills and could help maintain the tables. Haigh and young McSwan quickly became close friends. They were equally dressy types. McSwan's pencil moustache was trimmed as neatly as Haigh's clipped lip. The two shared a love of fast cars, expensive restaurant meals and convivial evenings in pubs. Haigh worked hard and well for the McSwan family for 18 months, and saved enough money to branch out on his own in 1937.

But not as an arcade manager. As a solicitor: as three solicitors, actually. He had devised an ingenious confidence trick. He had letterheads made up in the names of three imaginary solicitors' firms: one in Hastings, one in Guildford and one in Chancery Lane, London, each placed at an accommodation address where Haigh could receive mail. He studied the stock market and identified companies that were sound investments but vulnerable to a sudden offloading of their shares. He examined the company registers and identified shareholders with substantial holdings in them. Then he wrote on the solicitors' letterheads claiming to be a family lawyer instructed to dispose of a large holding of shares owned by a recently deceased stockholder, and offering to sell privately at a favourable price rather than depress the stock by putting it on the market. The scam worked. A quantity of large cheques started flowing in to the bogus solicitors' firms, and Haigh had only to bank them in the firms' names, and then close the accounts and run before anybody asked why their share certificates hadn't reached them.

But he had overlooked one dreadful mistake. The printer producing the Guildford letterhead had accidentally omitted the "d" in "Guildford" in the firm's telephone number. One shareholder spotted this and, doubting whether a legitimate solicitor would have let such a misprint pass, informed the police. Haigh was caught redhanded opening letters at the Guildford accommodation address. He had raised £3,000, but only had time to spend £240 of it. He was sentenced to four years' hard labour, first at Chelmsford Prison and then on Dartmoor.

There he read in prison-library law books that bringing a murder case depended on producing the *corpus delicti*, Latin for "body of the crime". Haigh believed that this meant there could be no indictment for murder unless a corpse that could be identified as the victim was found. He was quite wrong: the phrase describes the body of evidence that a crime has occurred, not the cadaver of the victim. But Haigh could not be dissuaded. And it is extremely probable that back in 1933 he had read the widespread newspaper accounts of a French lawyer called Sarret who had used sulphuric acid to reduce the body of a man he murdered to unrecognizable sludge.

Haigh was released on licence in 1940, but did not enjoy his liberty for long. An Italian woman for whom he offered to sell a refrigerator accused him of short-changing her, and complained to the police. Still on parole, he was sentenced to a further 21 months' hard labour. And in Lincoln Prison he conducted some experiments that pointed to the career he had in mind for himself. He stole quantities of acid from the prison tinsmith's shop, and from the batteries that worked bells in the prison. He stole jam jars from the kitchen. He bribed fellow convicts working on outdoor parties to bring him back field mice. And he found that the entire body of a mouse – bones, teeth and whiskers – could be dissolved if it was left in acid for long enough.

Haigh was 34 when he returned to the free world in 1943. He was liable for conscription, but ignored the recurrent summonses to medical examinations, and moved to new lodgings as each arrived. He answered a newspaper advertisement for a salesman and book-keeper, and thus made the acquaintance of Crawley and of Mr Alan Stephens.

Crawley, now the nearest town to Gatwick Airport, was just a village of a couple of thousand souls in those days. Villagers went to Horsham if they wanted to see a film or eat at a restaurant other than the local hotel, The George, or Ye Olde Ancient Priors teashop. Everybody knew everybody. Everybody knew Alan Stephens, a Welshman whose light-industrial firm made dolls' prams and similar fancy goods, and who won some useful war contracts to make radio components. "Steve", as the village knew Stephens, seemed a bit withdrawn to young Ron Shaw, a lifelong Crawley resident who still remembers all the people and events of the 1940s. But then, by the time Alan Stephens left the village to go back to Wales in 1949, he had every reason to retreat into his shell. Overcoming his suspicion of a suitor for his daughter who was 20 years older than the girl, he had nearly let her contract a bigamous marriage to a dreadful murderer.

None of this could have been foreseen in 1944. Haigh kept Stephens's books for him and, as he had done for the McSwans, worked honestly, loyally and well. There was enough work for him to make frequent stays at The George. His unusually smartly dressed figure became a familiar sight, as did his succession of super-smart cars. He had a Lagonda when he came. Later the village learned it had been stolen and found pushed off Beachy Head. Later still they would learn that the "thief" was Haigh himself and the wreck was an insurance scam. He had an Alvis. Once he had a boxy old wreck of a car which the local lads christened "the hearse". But he really was a good engineer, and before long he had transformed it into a gleaming blue collector's item which he sold for a profit.

And, like the Industrious Apprentice of eighteenth-century legend, he won the heart of the boss's daughter. Barbara Stephens was just 15 when she first saw John Haigh. His twinkling blue eyes, warm smile and well-to-do appearance instantly attracted her. She was not the first schoolgirl to be bowled over by the sophistication and maturity of an older man. And her parents, correctly sensing that Haigh was no lecherous seducer, did not object too seriously as she grew a little older and he started taking her out in the evenings. To the pictures in Horsham; to classical concerts at the Wigmore Hall in London. Their pleasures were innocent. There was not a hint of gossip about Barbara in the village. Nobody had any idea that Haigh was married to a wife he had practically never seen for 10 years, let alone that he had served three prison sentences for fraud. Barbara assumed they would get married when she was 21, and had Haigh lived that long they probably would have done and she would have continued to believe it incredible that he could have done the things he did.

Crawley was a village of independent light engineers. Ron Shaw did engineering work, and his father had been anodizing metals in the village in the previous generation. There was Tom Davies, who did a bit of welding. There was Edward Jones, whose Hurstlea Products made much the same sorts of fancy goods and components as Alan Stephens. And by the end of the war there was Haigh himself, working independently as Union Group Engineering.

The young lads of the village were uncomfortable with Haigh's townie dress and manners. Instead of drinking beer and whisky with them and their macho elders in the White Hart he held court drinking wine and sherry with those who would talk about music, opera and ballet in the Brewery Shades opposite The George. Some people called Haigh a spiv. His lemon gloves were almost an affront to rustic sensibilities. More psychoanalytically insightful than he may have realized, Ron Shaw thought it was "as if he was afraid of getting his hands dirty", and criticized him for being "always dressed up as if ... going to a party or something ... not a man ... bit of a poof, actually, I should say then".

After about a year Haigh gave up working for Alan Stephens. He had saved enough to rent a small basement off Gloucester Road, London, not far from the underground station, as his workshop. He took a bedsitting room in Queen's Gate Terrace: Kensington and Hammersmith were always his preferred part of London. When funds were good, he spent the odd night at the nearby Onslow Court Hotel, a largely residential establishment populated by rich old ladies with private means. The clean white linen damask napery, silver cutlery and crystal glasses suited Haigh to a T. His charm won over most of the residents, and they accepted his account of himself as a company director with an engineering degree who was constantly at work inventing marketable patented products.

And indeed, at this time he really was trying very hard to come up with a device that might make him a legitimate fortune. At the end of his life he was working on an adjustable coat-hanger that proved sufficiently serviceable for the clothing firm Gor-Ray to take it up and perfect it after his death.

But Haigh's name would not be remembered for his inventions. In the late summer of 1944 he dropped into The Goat in Kensington High Street for a glass of wine, when who should breeze in but his old friend and former employer William McSwan. Haigh said that he was doing well as an engineer and patentee with interests in Crawley and a small workshop in London. The McSwan family's pinball arcades had prospered until they sold all but one and converted the money into residential property in various parts of London. "Mac", as Haigh called his friend, had found the

Jack the Ripper: PC Neil finds Mary Ann Nichols' body in Buck's Row

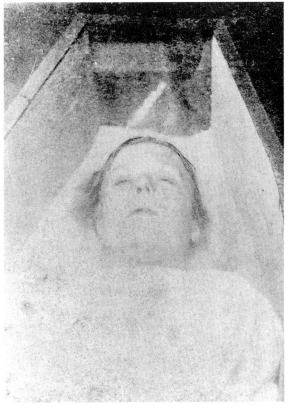

Mary Ann Nichols in Whitechapel Mortuary

Annie Chapman in the mortuary

Mary Jane Kelly's room
at 13 Miller's Court

Death, clothed like Mary Jane Kelly's last known
client and carrying his oilcloth package, accom-
panies her (imaginatively drawn in a hat she
never wore) to her door

Archie and Rosalie Henderson, the second couple Haigh
killed and dissolved

Police produce the oil drum in which Mrs Durand-Deacon
was dissolved at Crawley

The yard and Haigh's workshop in Crawley

Haigh remains smiling and friendly as police escort him to
Horsham magistrates' court

Detective Sergeant Patrick Heslin (left) and Divisional
Detective Inspector Shelley Symes (centre) arrive at
Horsham magistrates' court to attend Haigh's trial

Christie, the picture of respectability

The wash-house at 10 Rillington Place, where Christie hid
Beryl and Jeraldine Evans's bodies

Beryl Evans, the upstairs
neighbour Christie killed

Carrying a body out of 10 Rillington Place

The world's press gathers in Rillington Place

Timothy Evans, startled by a press photographer's flash
bulb, as police escort him off the train from Wales at
Paddington Station

Self-pitying Christie covers his face as he is brought
into court

Over: Bystanders and press photographers watch a Black Maria
convey Christie away from West Kensington Magistrates' Court

Tourists pose for snapshots outside 10 Rillington Place
before its demolition

advantages of becoming a *rentier* and was now collecting rent from a number of houses, which supported him and his parents comfortably. The remaining arcade had lain idle since the outbreak of war and they could not find a buyer for the machines. Haigh wondered whether he might be able to help, as he knew people who were interested in buying machinery.

He visited the elder McSwans in their new Pimlico flat: they had been bombed out of their home in Beckenham. They, like William, were happy to see him again. This trusting family had no idea that their former employee was a thrice-convicted fraudster, probably engaged at the time in some sort of investment and insurance scams to support his way of life.

Mac and John shared one problem: both were liable for conscription. Like Haigh, Mac had originally been exempt, partly on compassionate grounds as his business supported his parents. But now all able-bodied men were required, and Mac seems to have said something that gave Haigh appalling ideas.

"I shall have to disappear," he remarked.

Haigh idly wondered whether he had thought of going to Scotland. He had contacts there, he said, and could arrange for Mac to go to ground. But it was not to arrange for him to go to Scotland that Haigh invited the young man to visit his basement workshop in Gloucester Road. On Friday September 9 the two were enjoying a couple of glasses of wine and a pub meal in The Goat when Mac mentioned his concern that the pinball machines were deteriorating unsold. Haigh promptly offered to show him his basement workshop, just one tube stop away. It was after 10 o'clock when the two made their way through the blacked-out streets to the basement back entry at 79 Stanhope Mews. McSwan was looking at something that seemed to be part of a blowlamp when his host approached him from behind and felled him with a savage blow to the back of the head from a piece of lead pipe. Two more blows to the inert body ensured that McSwan was dead. John George Haigh, fraudster, had become a murderer.

Then, very calmly, he stripped the body of its valuables: watch, money and papers; washed the bloodstains off the floor, covered the body with a blanket and went back to his bedsitting room in Queen's Gate Terrace.

After breakfast the next morning he went out to search the neighbourhood for a container, and found an oil drum used by Air Raid Protection volunteers as a water butt. Borrowing a handcart from a builder's yard, he pushed the unwieldy vessel to Stanhope Mews. There was nothing unusual about a well-dressed man pushing junk in a handcart in wartime. Petrol rationing prohibited the use of cars for private purposes, and the turning over of manufacturing to war matériel made all manner of odds and ends valuable to the householder.

Then Haigh performed a remarkable feat. Ron Shaw recollects that "those 45-gallon oil drums that we used to use then, they've got two ribs round them, which are meant for rolling them along the road ... You used to roll them up a little, on to a wood staging, and roll it round so that you put a tap in the end and rolled it over 180 degrees with a tap in it. Now, for anyone to turn that upright – it's impossible for one person, when it's full of oil, to even tip it upright. It used to take two or three, if you tried, and it was a very risky business."

Nonetheless, Haigh contrived to double up William McSwan's body and force it into the oil drum before forcing it into an upright position. It took him over half an hour, and there was a worse job to come.

For some reason, he was keeping 30 gallons of hydrochloric and sulphuric acid in the basement. This was far more than he needed for stripping metals, and this fact, coupled with his experiments on mice in Lincoln Prison, forces the conclusion that he anticipated the possibility of murder long before the opportunity arose. Industrial acid was kept in 10-gallon carboys: large, round glass flasks resting on straw nests in metal stands. (Haigh's crimes added this rather specialist noun to newspaper readers' vocabularies.) It was impossible for Haigh to lift a carboy and tip its contents over the edge of the oil drum. So, donning heavy rubber gloves, boots and apron to protect himself against serious burns, he poured the liquid into a bucket and then emptied the bucket over Mac's body. It took hours to cover the corpse, and the process nearly killed Haigh. As the acid reacted with flesh it rose to a temperature of 300°F and gave off choking, toxic fumes. Haigh had to break off repeatedly and rush outside for gulps of fresh air. But he persevered all day until the body was completely immersed. And he left the unbelievable horror-comic setting he had created, and went back home to rest for 24 hours.

He found, on his return, that a human body in an oil drum took longer to dissolve than a mouse's body in a jam jar. Most of Mac had turned to thick, stinking sludge. But there were bony and fatty lumps in the bottom of the drum. Still, they were small enough to be poured away down the drain in the centre of the basement. William McSwan was washed away through the sewers and out to the Thames estuary. There was, Haigh wrongly believed, no *corpus delicti*, and so, in law, no murder.

This was the *modus operandi* that made Haigh unique among serial killers. It was what he did next that proved him a master criminal. He went to McSwan's parents and told them that William had gone to Scotland to evade his army call-up. He used McSwan's keys to enter his flat, steal his clothes and take away personal papers from which he could master the forging of Mac's handwriting. He paid off the rent, telling the landlord that McSwan would be away for some time. Then he took the night train to Scotland and post-ed a forged letter from McSwan to his parents. He did this repeatedly for the next nine months, as he kept up the pretence that William McSwan was alive and well and hiding out from the army. He took an accommodation address in Glasgow in McSwan's name, and cashed the generous allowance that the elder McSwans sent him. He wrote a letter from "William" suggesting that John Haigh might save Mrs McSwan the labour of collecting the rents on the family's properties. The offer was taken up, and Haigh familiarized himself with the details of the McSwans' real estate. He went to a solicitor with the murdered man's identity card and other papers, and claimed to be William McSwan. He had the solicitor draw up a Power of Attorney over his affairs so that his friend John George Haigh could manage everything for him. He went to another solicitor as John George Haigh, and had the Power of Attorney activated. He started selling the pinball machines, honestly reporting to Mr and Mrs McSwan that he was doing so. It was an astonishing feat of protracted fraud and forgery.

But it depended on the war's continuing. After VE Day the McSwans expected the return of their son to London. On the morning of July 6, 1945 Haigh acted. He asked Donald McSwan to come to the Gloucester Road basement to give him a hand with renovating one of the pinball machines. The old man agreed. He was killed instantaneously with an iron bar that smashed the back of his head as soon as he was inside the workshop. Haigh purloined his watch, wallet and papers, trussed the body like a roasting fowl and stuffed it into a new oil drum he had acquired. In the afternoon he went back to the flat in Pimlico and told Amy McSwan that her husband had been taken faint and was sitting in his workshop recovering with a cup of tea. As he had calculated, Mrs McSwan insisted on being taken to Gloucester Road immediately. There she was dispatched like her husband, and stuffed into a second oil drum. For filling the acid baths this time, Haigh had acquired a stirrup pump. With its support leg removed, it could be placed directly into a carboy and he could pump the liquid straight into the drums. Where one drum had taken him a day to fill by bucket, two were now filled in an evening.

Haigh had also fashioned a crude mask to protect himself from the fumes. This was less successful. But after 48 hours the McSwans had turned to sludge, and were poured down the drain to disappear for ever through the sewers.

With his Power of Attorney, Haigh secured all William's property. He forged a deed, transferring to William ownership of one house that was in Amy's name. He told the McSwans' landlady and neighbours that they had been called to America suddenly. He was extremely lucky that no one was close enough to the family to doubt him. The London County Council was puzzled when Donald ceased to draw his pension, and two officials came round to see what was happening. When they were redirected to Haigh, he offered them a forwarding address, where he himself continued to draw the old man's money. He renewed the family's ration books, giving himself a useful quadruple allocation of food and clothing. He sold off their houses and belongings, raising at least £3,000. He gave up his bedsitter, and installed himself as a resident in the Onslow Court Hotel.

He was now living the luxurious life he had always wanted. He charmed the old ladies at the hotel, and delighted them with his piano playing. He used some of the McSwans' money for experiments with elaborate toys to be produced by a new manufacturing friend in London, but the electric kiddie car he designed was rejected by toyshops because he made it too fast to be safe, and he never completed the army of toy soldiers which should have marched themselves along a complicated system of clockwork pulleys. He was a regular visitor to the Wigmore Hall, and was delighted to be introduced to the concert pianist Albert Ferber at dinner with his toy-manufacturer friend. He became friendly with Edward Jones in

Crawley, a light-engineering manufacturer like Alan Stephens, whose success made him seem to local youth Ron Shaw "a bit of a wide boy". That would be no disrecommendation to Haigh, who volunteered to be the unpaid, unofficial London representative for Jones's Hurstlea Products. He celebrated this "appointment" by describing himself as a Director of Hurstlea: a simple piece of self-promotion for a man whose letterhead already awarded him an unearned BSc. When Hurstlea outgrew its small brick workshop in Giles Yard, Leopold Road, and moved to a disused factory in West Street in 1947, Haigh was allowed to use the old building for "experiments".

But he was still not satisfied. He wanted more money. And he was confident that, with his intelligence, he could make it by applying mathematical probabilities to the movement of horses. He worked out an infallible "system" to beat the bookmakers. And, with mathematical infallibility, he lost all his money very quickly. By September 1947 he was overdrawn at the bank, where he had recently held £5,000. He owed £400 on his latest motor car, and the Onslow Court Hotel was pressing him to pay his bill. It was time for him to make another killing.

He started with a return to real estate dealing. A house in Ladbroke Square, Notting Hill, was advertised in the newspapers. Haigh answered the advertisement, viewed the house and told the vendor he would be happy to take it, only the price of £8,750 was too low. Fifty-two-year-old Dr Archie Henderson, a veteran of the Highland Brigade in the First World War and the Royal Army Medical Corps in the Second World War, was surprised and delighted when the dapper company director insisted that he couldn't dream of offering less than £10,500. Archie's wife, Rosalie, was still more delighted, says her nephew, Martin Burlin. "Rose was gushing. She said, 'Oh, I've met this wonderful man!… He's told me I'm not asking enough for the business; I should ask for another

£5,000.'" The "business", however, was not for sale. It was a toyshop with flats above in Dawes Road, Fulham, which traded as the Dolls' Hospital. With a manageress to run the shop and themselves installed in one of the flats, this was the Hendersons' new venture after they sold the Ladbroke Square house (not, of course, to Haigh). Martin Burlin was not yet born when his aunt and uncle met Haigh, and Sussex journalist David Briffett, who has studied the Haigh case in more depth than anyone else alive, was given a completely different impression by Arnold Burlin, Rosalie's brother and Martin's father. According to Arnold, Archie was overwhelmed by Haigh. But Rosalie, a much more shrewd business-woman, thought him completely stupid for offering an inflated price, and more or less shared her brother's opinion that "When you meet a man who talks like that, you should run for your life." To their cost, Archie and Rosalie did not run.

Haigh's offer to buy the house had led nowhere except to an increasing friendship with the Hendersons. He played the piano for them, and impressed them with his sophisticated pleasure in exotic French dishes like *tête de veau*. Archie shared his love of racing, and the two went to Ascot together. And Archie was taken down to Crawley and shown around Hurstlea, where he had a long conversation with Jones and Haigh about the possibility of investing money in a new powder compact the company was developing. As Haigh learned when Archie expanded over a bottle of whisky, Rosalie might not altogether approve. Archie had inherited £20,000 from his first wife, who died tragically, and he enjoyed a lucrative medical practice in west London. But Rosalie did not think he managed his money well, and there were rows about it.

Haigh took in everything. He took in, too, Archie's possession of two wartime souvenirs that he could use: an officer's .38 Enfield revolver with an envelope of bullets, and a service gas mask.

In February 1948 the Hendersons decided on a short holiday: a long weekend at Broadstairs and Brighton. Casually, Haigh suggested that he might drop in for tea with them at the Metropole Hotel in Brighton when he was working at Crawley. Once they had left for Broadstairs, Haigh turned up at their flat and told their housekeeper, Miss Daisy Rowntree, that Archie had asked him to pick up some things and take them down to the Metropole. Miss Rowntree believed him, and Haigh left with the leather hatbox in which Archie kept his pistol as well as some personal papers.

On Wednesday February 11 Haigh paid his promised visit to the Metropole, and persuaded Archie to set aside Friday for a visit to Crawley to have a look at the Leopold Road works. Rosalie would not accompany them: the family tradition, as passed down to Martin Burlin, was that she was intensely superstitious and would never travel anywhere on a Friday the 13th. Unfortunately for her she let a crisis override superstition when the day came.

Archie and Haigh drove to Crawley in the morning and lunched at The George. Then they trundled over to the workshop in Leopold Road, where Haigh shot Archie through the back of the head with his own pistol. It was 2.15 when he leaped into his car and drove like a fury to Dawes Road. There he told Miss Rowntree that he had yet more items to collect for Dr Henderson, and made off with the gas mask. He raced back to Crawley with it, stopping on the way at Tom Davies's works to pick up one of two 45-gallon oil drums he had ordered from him. Then, with the gas mask and oil drum stashed in the workshop, and Archie's body in the oil drum, Haigh drove on to Brighton.

It was dark when he reached Rosalie, waiting irritably in the foyer of the Metropole. She was annoyed to learn that Archie was feeling unwell and resting at a neighbour's house; annoyed enough to swallow Haigh's improbable claim that he thought it would be better for him to come and tell her in person and fetch her, rather than telephoning and letting her come by taxi to Crawley. This moment of naivety always surprised her family. A shrewd businesswoman who had helped her brother run nightclubs before the war, she seemed too wordly-wise to have fallen for Haigh's flannel. But fall she did, and went back to Crawley with him, accepting his excuse that he had to pick up some things from Leopold Road and agreeing to his request to come in to help him carry them, only to be shot in the back of the head and left overnight under a piece of sacking next to the oil drum holding her husband. Haigh took her wedding ring and diamond engagement ring. He took Archie's gold pocket watch, gold cigarette case and wallet. He packed up the gun and its holster in the hatbox, and went to a telephone to call the Metropole. The Hendersons had been travelling with their red setter, Pat. Adopting a high voice and posing as Rosalie, he asked the hotel to look after Pat and walk him in the morning, as they would be out overnight. Then he drove home to the Onslow Court Hotel.

His acid-bath methods were now almost perfected. He collected his second oil drum from Tom Davies, and with the gas mask as well as the stirrup pump, made relatively easy work of inundating the Hendersons. Emptying away the sludge two days later was not quite so easy. There was no drain in the workshop, and he had to carry out bucketfuls to the yard and throw them among the rubble and litter. Although a recognizable undissolved foot clumped out of Archie's drum, he simply dumped it among the nettles, and a year later it had completely disappeared as the acid on it went on working.

The hardest part of this crime was reassuring Mrs Henderson's brother. The Burlins had noted with some surprise that Haigh had come to completely dominate the Hendersons' social life. Other friends, like Miss Rowntree the housekeeper, were surprised by the information that Archie and Rosalie had travelled on to Scotland and might be going abroad without returning, but believed Haigh. He took over Pat, who became his pet for six months. But Arnold

Burlin mistrusted Haigh, and could not believe that this recent acquaintance had been entrusted with settling up all their affairs and sending on or disposing of all their property. He could not imagine why Rosalie had not telephoned him about her plans, and when Haigh said he was taking over the Dolls' Hospital, Burlin became seriously obstructive. He had lent Rosalie money recently, with the Dawes Road property as collateral. But the agreement between brother and sister had been made without benefit of lawyers. Haigh forged a Deed of Transfer making over the property to himself, and forged a further letter from Rosalie explaining to Arnold that he had been very good to them and lent them money, and she had to let him have it.

When Burlin still threatened to go to the police if he didn't see Rosalie in person, Haigh invented new stories, backed up with letters purportedly from her. First she explained that the couple's marriage was at breaking point over Archie's mismanagement of money, and so they had gone to the country alone to sort it out. Then she confirmed a story that Burlin had not believed from Haigh: that Archie had carried out an abortion and the police were after him. And when she wrote a long letter from South Africa, full of family phrases and intimate personal recollections (which Haigh had picked up from the Hendersons' purloined correspondence and papers), Burlin was convinced that his sister was alive and abroad, if behaving utterly uncharacteristically.

Haigh had made about £6,000 from the murder of the McSwans, and it supported him from 1943 to 1947. He made about £7,000 from the murder of the Hendersons (worth, say, 40 times as much at today's values) and threw it away after horses and dogs within six months. Hence the relative desperation of his last murder, and its tiny haul.

Mrs Olive Durand-Deacon sat at the table next to Haigh's in the dining-room of the Onslow Court Hotel. A widow with £36,000 invested to keep her comfortably, she probably attracted his attention as a possible source of large sums in the long run. But with the hotel, the bank, bookmakers and personal friends who had lent him money all pressing him, he couldn't afford to wait. In February 1949 the elderly lady put her head into a noose. She had seen some artificial fingernails for sale and discussed them over lunch with her friend Mrs Birin, secretary of the Bacon Society. (Mrs Durand-Deacon held one firm and irrational belief: the popular delusion that Francis Bacon wrote the works of William Shakespeare.) When Haigh sat down at his table she leaned over and proposed to him that he might think about manufacturing a new design. The fly had just walked itself into the spider's parlour. Haigh didn't react overeagerly. He said he'd think it over for a few days. He went back to his room and drew up a sinister shopping list:

Drum
Enamelling brush
H_2SO_4
Paint brush
Stirrup pump
Gloves
Apron
Rags
Cotton wool pad
Some red paper.

It was a list of requisites for murder. The acids had corroded his equipment, which needed replacing. He intended to paint the inside of his next oil drum with enamel to resist the acid and make it reusable. In the event he was able to buy a drum that was already enamelled. Either way, it proved that this man intended to murder again after killing Mrs Durand-Deacon.

On Thursday, February 17 everything was ready. At dinner that night, Haigh invited Mrs Durand-Deacon to go to Crawley with him the following day to look at his work. Making the appointment as late as possible, he also suggested that she keep it a secret for commercial reasons. Haigh's hope, of course, was that no one should know he ever saw her on Friday.

On Friday morning Haigh hurried down to Crawley, helped Jones shift some sheet metal from Leopold Road to West Street, pocketed the Leopold Road keys and reminded Jones that he was bringing a potential investor down in the afternoon to discuss fingernails. Thus he was prepared, should the occasion arise, to say he had intended to meet Mrs Durand-Deacon, but she hadn't turned up.

After lunch Mrs Durand-Deacon went to the Army & Navy Stores in Victoria Street. Haigh left the hotel separately from her and picked her up outside the shop. They drove to Crawley, where Mrs Durand-Deacon discreetly asked if she could go to a cloak-room. Haigh put her down at the George and went in separately himself, unaware that the hotel bookkeeper, to whom he was a familiar figure, saw the old lady in the Persian lamb coat leave the hotel and get into his car with him. Haigh went straight on to Leopold Road. In the workshop he pointed Mrs Durand-Deacon to "some red paper" on which he had sketched outlines, and while she looked at it he shot her through the back of the head. His pad of cotton wool mopped up nearly all the blood, and he didn't notice that there was a tiny spray of drops on the wall. He went to West Street and told Jones that the investor hadn't turned up. He went back to Leopold Road and removed Mrs Durand-Deacon's pearl necklace, earrings, finger rings, wristwatch and gold crucifix. He searched her red plastic handbag, appropriating 30 shillings and a fountain pen. He trussed the body and put it in the oil drum, tossing the handbag after it. He kept the Persian lamb coat on a bench, to be cleaned before he sold it. He took Mrs Durand-Deacon's property and the hatbox containing Archie's pistol out to his car. While doing so, he was observed by a lorry driver who always left his vehicle overnight in Giles Yard. Then, feeling peckish, Haigh stopped work and went for a poached egg at Ye Olde Ancient Priors teashop, engaging in jocular conversation with the manager while he had his tea.

Back to work he went after tea, donning his rubber protective gear and gas mask before pumping more than 10 gallons of acid on the body. And then he dined at the George before driving back to Kensington to sleep the sleep of the just at the Onslow Court Hotel.

He had a shock at breakfast time. Mrs Constance Lane, another resident and a good friend of Olive Durand-Deacon, was concerned about that lady's disappearance. She hadn't been in to dinner the night before. She wasn't down to breakfast, and the chambermaid said her bed hadn't been slept in. Now, she had gone out to meet John the previous afternoon to see his factory in Crawley, hadn't she? So where was she now? Haigh must inwardly have cursed the loose tongues of old ladies. But if Olive had left the hotel telling Constance where she was going, it would be folly to say he knew nothing about it. He produced the story he had already planted on Edward Jones. She just hadn't turned up. And Haigh pretended to be concerned. It wouldn't be safe or sensible to dissolve Mrs Lane. But he would keep an eye on her.

He was very busy that day. He had Mrs Durand-Deacon's jewellery to be valued, her wristwatch to sell and her fur coat to take to the cleaners. And her body to be given a stir. While he was out, the Onslow Court buzzed with Olive's disappearance. And when Haigh asked Mrs Lane if she'd heard anything about her friend on Sunday morning, she told him that after lunch she was going to report Olive to the police as a missing person. Haigh offered to go with her. It has been said that Mrs Lane didn't much like Haigh, but she jumped at the offer of a lift in his car. The two went to Chelsea Police Station, where the desk sergeant made a note of their report, but had little expectation of its amounting to anything. Mrs Durand-Deacon had lived 10 years as a widow without doing anything sillier than believing Bacon wrote Shakespeare. Unless there had been a road accident, she was as likely as not to have taken herself off on her own affairs. Nothing would be done until the following day.

Haigh's nemesis, Woman Police Sergeant Alexandra Lambourne, received the dull duty of following up the report on Monday morning. Hospitals and accident report checks quickly established that the old lady had not been run over. Sergeant Lambourne went to the Onslow Court Hotel to interview the pair who had reported Mrs Durand-Deacon's absence. And Sergeant Lambourne immediately jumped to the right suspicion: not by forensic science or psychological profiling. She used the good old policeman's "hunch", which comes from long experience of interviewing a mix of "wrong 'uns" and "right 'uns", and which psychologist Professor David Canter of Liverpool University and his associate Rupert Heritage hope to analyse into explicable and demonstrable fragments of subliminal observation. Because Sergeant Lambourne was a woman, conventionally minded observers talked about "woman's intuition". But there was straightforward detective common sense in her first observation that since nothing but Mrs Durand-Deacon's handbag and fur coat had been taken out of room, the old lady had not intended to travel far or stay out overnight. There was sensible knowledge of the world in Sergeant Lambourne's seeing a well-groomed, hard-working 39-year-old company director as peculiarly out of place in the company of geriatric old ladies living off their investments. And something just seemed wrong about Haigh's charming helpfulness. On her routine report to CID saying that she had found out nothing, Sergeant Lambourne added a personal memorandum that it seemed worth checking up on this John George Haigh who was somehow in the middle of the story.

Divisional Detective Inspector Shelley Symes did not dismiss this as female silliness. He ran a preliminary check with the Criminal Records Office at Scotland Yard. And to his astonishment he learned that the innocent-sounding civilian was a highly experienced confidence trickster.

The rest of the week represented a race between the police trying to find out what Haigh was up to and Haigh trying to cover his tracks. Inspectors Shelley Symes and Albert Webb in Chelsea enlisted the aid of West Sussex Constabulary's Detective Inspector Pat Heslin to interview Haigh's associates in Crawley and search Hurstlea Products' West Street premises. Edward Jones feared that Haigh had been black-marketeering and would bring discredit on his company. But all the police learned was that Haigh drew no salary from his "directorship" of Hurstlea. He did not reassure them of his honesty when he smilingly agreed and claimed to make money at the racetracks.

Haigh still had to empty the dissolved remains of Mrs Durand-Deacon (including some bits of bone and fat, and the remains of her handbag) into the rubble-strewn corner of Giles Yard; sell some of her jewellery; and shift the incriminating hatbox containing Archie Henderson's pistol from his car boot back to Leopold Road once the police had completed their enquiries at Hurstlea. And he had a new problem that required another mass murder. Mrs Burlin, Rosalie Henderson's mother, was critically ill, and Arnold was horrified that approaches through Haigh failed to elicit any response from his sister. He expected her to return to England immediately, and arranged for an emergency SOS message to be broadcast by the BBC. He told Haigh he would be coming down to London from Manchester the following Monday and going to

Scotland Yard. Haigh, who had retained the best possible relations with the Burlins, sending a silver spoon and pusher as christening gifts when baby Martin was born, was sympathetic and supportive. He promised to arrange accommodation in London for the whole family, and, as the Burlins subsequently realized, probably planned to eliminate them.

Fifty years later it emerged for the first time how he set about improving his technique and equipment. Brook Lapping Productions, preparing a television programme on Haigh, interviewed Ron Shaw, and learned about a previously unknown commission that Tom Davies undertook for Haigh. Shaw went to do some repairs on Davies's van and found Davies "struggling ... with some big sheets of metal about ... 5 foot 6 long, about ... 15 inches high and about 15 inches wide, and he said, 'Just hold this, Ron, will you while I tack it.' So I held it while he tacked it all up into a ... box, and then he said that it was got to be painted with acid-proof paint, because it's for old John Haigh ... who was going to do some anodizing." Neither Davies nor Shaw thought there was anything odd about Haigh's wanting a long bath for the acid treatment of long metal objects. Both knew that oil drums of the kind Haigh had previously acquired from Davies were unwieldy and dangerous as acid baths. But once Haigh had been exposed, Shaw had no doubt at all that the custom-built bath was intended for people: indeed, he assumed that it had been used to dispose of Mrs Durand-Deacon, unaware that the police had found the treated oil drum Haigh used for her dissolution.

Haigh's downfall came on the Saturday. Inspector Heslin was severely overworked as he had to deal with the concurrent case of the worst sort of police "rotten apple": a local sergeant who had been caught red-handed as the perpetrator of a series of burglaries. Nevertheless he decided to pay one more visit to Edward Jones, and asked him whether Hurstlea had any other premises. Jones told him about the Leopold Road workshop and its use by Haigh, and Heslin immediately telephoned Symes and won his approval for a search. Since Haigh had retained the keys, Heslin had to break in. The gas mask, rubber protective clothing, stirrup pump and carboys of acid aroused no suspicion. They were plausible engineer's equipment. But an attaché case initialled "JGH" and a hatbox labelled "H" held mysterious contents. The attaché case contained ration books, identity cards and other personal papers in the names of Donald, Amy and William McSwan. And in the hatbox a similar collection of papers were in the names of Dr Archie and Mrs Rosalie Henderson. These evidently lay behind some sort of fraud. But at this point the police hadn't the faintest idea who these people were. They were beginning to suspect that Haigh might have done away with Mrs Durand-Deacon. They didn't have an inkling that she was his sixth murder victim.

Evidence relating to murder lay in the bottom of the hatbox. Archie Henderson's Enfield revolver, and an envelope containing silver bullets. The science of forensic ballistics had been greatly advanced by consultant gunsmith Robert Churchill in the interwar period. His comparison microscope (though originally disparaged by CID chief Sir Wyndham Childs) proved invaluable in establishing whether a given bullet had been fired from a given gun. None of Haigh's spent bullets survived his acid baths. But ballistics was able to establish that the pistol in the hatbox had been fired within the past week. Haigh was now in for serious questioning at Chelsea Police Station.

To the astonishment of Symes and Webb, the suave fraudster who had hitherto explained away everything now confessed immediately. He opened by saying that although he had killed Mrs Durand-Deacon, the police would never be able to prove it as he had dissolved the body in acid, and nothing remained. He went on to tell the astonished officers all about the McSwans and the Hendersons.

While Symes was out of the room, he casually asked Webb what were the chances of getting out of Broadmoor. And that calculation that he might claim to be insane most probably explains the exotically gruesome touch he added to his confession. In every murder, he said, he had used a penknife to sever the victim's carotid artery and drain off a glass of blood, which he drank. He explained that he had long suffered nightmares of travelling through a forest in rain which turned to blood as the trees turned to crucifixes, and he knew that his only escape was to drink a cup of blood that was tantalizingly impossible to reach when a crucified man held it out to him. Soon after these dreams started, he claimed, he had felt under a compulsion to drink his own urine – though nobody ever saw him do so. He described a motor accident when his car hit a lorry as he was driving back to London after taking Barbara Stephens out one night. (This accident certainly occurred.) He was briefly concussed, he said, and came to to find blood trickling down his face and into his mouth. Its taste made an indelible impression on him and left him with a craving to drink more. And that was the real motive for his murders.

The police thought that money supplied a perfectly comprehensible motive in every case. And Haigh was smart enough to spot this weakness. Four days later he volunteered a further confession. Now he claimed three more victims: a young woman he picked up in Hammersmith in February 1945, and whose name he did not remember; a young man called Max whom he picked up in The Goat that autumn; and a black-haired woman called Mary whom he met on the promenade in Eastbourne in the autumn of 1948. Here were three killings with no mercenary motive: only the blood-drinking. The police had no doubt that he made them up. The author Colin Wilson has pointed out that blood is an emetic, but Haigh never mentioned having vomited after his enormities.

Haigh was wrong to think there was no physical evidence linking him to the crime. The pathologist, Dr Simpson, went to Giles Yard, and immediately spotted a human gallstone in the sludge. Forensic pathologists today differ as to whether this was a brilliant piece of perception or something that nobody competent could have missed. Simpson had the sludge gathered up and sifted, and recovered a piece of pelvis which proved the body to have been female; foot bones which could be reconstructed into a foot that fitted Mrs Durand-Deacon's shoe; and, most important, her dentures and the remains of her handbag, which positively identified her.

The newspapers were quickly on to the sensational story. Details of Haigh's confession leaked from the police, and the *Daily Mirror* went too far in printing screaming headlines about the "Vampire Killer". Metropolitan Police Commissioner Sir Harold Scott, the canny former civil servant who devised the phrase "helping the police with their enquiries" to avoid infringing a perpetrator's right to the presumption of innocence, warned the newspapers three times that publishing data from confessions made under caution for which there was no other evidence risked contempt of court. The *Mirror* didn't tone down its stories far enough, and with the *News of the World* paying his legal expenses in return for his giving his life story to be published after his trial, Haigh sued. The court treated the case very seriously indeed, fining the paper £10,000, hauling its company directors into the dock for a severe wigging from Lord Chief Justice Goddard and sending the editor to prison for three months.

Yet when it came to his trial Haigh enthusiastically endorsed everything the *Mirror* had said. His lawyers' problem was finding a psychologist who would agree that these things had happened and Haigh was mad. Those who examined him all concluded he was sane. Finally Dr Henry Yellowlees concluded that he suffered from "pure paranoia" and would compulsively lead a Jekyll and Hyde life. Attorney-General Sir Hartley Shawcross, the prosecuting counsel, destroyed Yellowlees with two questions. Were all his conclusions based on things Haigh had said to him in three interviews? Was he aware that Haigh was a habitual liar?

That was the end of Haigh's defence. When the jury found him guilty, he insouciantly remarked, "It's no use crying over spilt milk" and returned his attention to completing his memoirs for Stafford Somerfield, the *News of the World* journalist who had befriended him. He arranged for Madame Tussaud's to receive his favourite green suit and socks to go on his effigy in the Chamber of Horrors. He joked about saying to God, after his hanging, "Sorry I dropped in like this." He left a deeply grieved Barbara Stephens, still unable to believe that he had killed so many people while making chaste and charming love to her.

David Briffett, after exhaustive study of the case, is impressed by the fact that Haigh's story about his nightmares and blood-drinking never changed from the first time he produced it: given the high qualifications and large experience Dr Yellowlees brought to the examination; and given the discovery of a penknife stained with human blood exactly where Haigh said he kept it, in the glove compartment of his car, Briffett suggests that there may be reasonable doubt about Haigh's sanity.

For most people, though, John George Haigh is the classic example of the calculating, materialistic serial killer.

1920–1960

THE PERIOD 1920 TO 1960 was a golden age for Scotland Yard's CID. Britain's supremacy in filing and retaining criminal records identifiable by fingerprints produced a highly successful rate of crime solution, and masked the fact that hitherto England had fallen behind France in the science of blood grouping and classification. The Locard principle, that every contact leaves a trace, was enunciated at the beginning of the century, and slowly the police came to see the virtue of collecting minute samples from crime sites and submitting them to microscopic examination. In 1935 clerk Sergeant Cyril Cuthbert, a keen amateur scientist, used microscopic and chemical tests to decipher the original writing on a document that had been tampered with, and won a commendation from the Chief Constable of Folkestone for his help. The short-sighted Assistant Commissioner of the Metropolitan Police, Sir Norman Kendall, reprimanded Cuthbert for exceeding his duties, but fortunately the Commissioner at the time was the flamboyantly independent Lord Trenchard, who demanded to see the

Metropolitan "Police Science Lab". There wasn't one, and Cuthbert had to be put in a white coat and planted among his flasks and test tubes to put on a show for the Commissioner. Trenchard immediately raised funds to start a proper forensic-science laboratory: the first in the country, the most up to date in the world at that time, and the ancestor of today's chain of Home Office Forensic Science centres. Cuthbert was appointed to liaise between the Met and the laboratory. With the rank of Superintendent, he oversaw the transfer of samples from Crawley to London in the investigation of Haigh's murders.

This was also the golden age of the "Murder Squad" – which did not actually exist under that name. But in 1924 Bernard Spilsbury, Dr Scott-Gillett and Superintendent Percy Savage really did devise the "murder bag": a cow-hide Gladstone, of which six were held in readiness at Scotland Yard, containing rubber gloves, weighing and measuring instruments, tweezers, magnifying glasses, containers for samples, fingerprinting equipment, writing equipment and everything else that two doctors and a detective could envisage would help a police officer at a scene of crime. The need for such gear became apparent when Spilsbury, to his horror, saw Savage risking sepsis by touching pieces of Miss Emily Kaye's decomposing flesh with his bare hands. The case was the Second Crumbles Murder. In that innocent "classic" period of British murder, several crimes achieved this sort of dynastic listing and placing: the First and Second Brighton Trunk Murders; the First and Second Potter's Bar Golf Course Murders; the Soho Silk Stocking Murders. Until his arrest, Christie's case featured in the papers as "The Notting Hill Murders".

JOHN REGINALD HALLIDAY CHRISTIE

Sensational as the "Acid Bath Murders" of Haigh were, John Reginald Halliday Christie's crimes evoked the greatest public shock since Jack the Ripper's. The Notting Hill Murders rather than the Whitechapel Murders established our contemporary thirst for crime with a lot of bodies and perverse sex. The Ripper was an extraordinary sport, his identity shrouded in the mystery of a slum rookery. Christie was the man next door in a terraced street, his exotic evil screaming out against its environment.

Christie was caught at the time when the character of "Dixon of Dock Green" (introduced in the 1949 film *The Blue Lamp*) was accepted as realistic. Retiring senior CID officers regularly regaled the public with their "Knacker of the Yard" reminiscences. Most Britons agreed that "our police are wonderful". The Christie case not only offered a delicious frisson of horror and nausea: re-examined by a true-crime writer who conducted a crusade for justice, it played a major part in undermining that good opinion of British police methods, and struck a mighty blow against capital punishment.

As the first stories reached the papers in March 1953, it was clear that these murders were something new. Number 10 Rillington Place, the little end house overshadowed by a brick wall and a foundry chimney, was the first murderer's "house of horrors" to be uncovered in England. "Three Women's Bodies Found in Notting Hill House!" was the first headline. "Another Body in Notting Hill!" followed hard on its tail. Then "Police Digging up Notting Hill Garden!" And, sure enough, they soon uncovered "Two More Bodies in Notting Hill!"

And, all the time, the repeated statement: "Police urgently wish to interview the former tenant, Mr John Reginald Halliday Christie." For a week the hunt for Christie dominated the news. He was not caught by successful detective investigation or remarkable forensic science. Good luck and basic beat patrolling uncovered him: the same elements that later caught Peter Sutcliffe, the Yorkshire Ripper. PC Thomas Ledger saw an unshaven vagrant loitering on Putney Bridge, was dissatisfied with the account he gave of himself and asked him to remove his hat. And with the unmistakable Christie dome revealed, he made the arrest.

It transpired that after leaving Notting Hill, Christie had stayed under his own name in King's Cross Road at one of the charitable hostels for homeless men erected with a bequest from Disraeli's private secretary, Lord Rowton. Thereafter he had wandered all over London, sleeping rough. But the police were not criticized for failing to arrest him sooner: they had been inundated with misinformation about supposed sightings.

The sequence of events leading to this manhunt was straightforward, if genuinely sensational. Charles Brown, the West Indian landlord of 10 Rillington Place, had been surprised to find a couple called Reilly occupying the ground-floor flat. The legal tenants were Mr and Mrs Reg Christie. They were the only remaining white occupants of the house: an unlovely racist couple who detested the

West Indian immigration into the neighbourhood and made their feelings known by pouring disinfectant in the corridor outside their rooms to demonstrate their conviction that black people were dirty. It was a bit rich coming from them. When Christie sold the furniture before taking a deposit and illegally subletting the flat to the Reillys, the dealer who went to the rooms found them a complete rat's nest, the mattress stained and full of bedbugs.

Charles Brown promptly evicted the Reillys and invited one of the upstairs tenants, Mr Beresford Brown (no relation to the landlord), to have the use of the Christies' rooms. Mr Beresford Brown was disconcerted to find the whole downstairs flat unpleasantly smelly. Tapping the kitchen walls to find a suitable point for fixing brackets to support a wireless, he found a place which sounded like hollow wood, and at one corner of this, a section where the paper didn't seem to rest on anything at all, he tore a little hole in the paper and flashed his torch inside. He was looking into a tiny alcove, 2 feet wide by 5 feet deep, that had once been used as a coalhole. But he was looking at the bare back of a half-naked woman's corpse. He rushed out of the house to call the police.

The body, dressed only in suspender belt, stockings, shortsleeved bolero, blouse and bra, was prevented from pitching forward on its face by the fact that the bra strap was tied to a taller bundle leaning against the wall. Between the body and this tall bundle was another bundle. This proved to contain another young woman's body, parcelled up in a blanket. And the tall bundle was a third young woman, also tied up in a blanket, resting on her back and shoulders with her legs propped up vertically. Some ashes had been loosely shovelled over her head, which was wrapped in a pillowcase. The police immediately summoned a pathologist.

Keith Simpson was not the only pathologist in London at this time. He had two rivals, Dr Donald Teare and Professor Francis Camps. According to Camps's assistant, Dr Bill Hunt, Teare was "a very nice chap, and he was probably the best of the three". Camps and Simpson, by contrast, "were very much prima donnas in those days". Camps and Simpson hated each other. Bill Hunt had no idea which of them was to blame. Camps hated anyone he considered a rival, including assistants like Hunt. He was, Hunt felt, the most egotistical man he had ever met – until he met Simpson.

The police and crime correspondents sometimes called Teare, Camps and Simpson "the three musketeers". The Christie case was the only one where all three were called in together to give an opinion. But that did not happen until Christie had been tried and convicted and was awaiting execution.

When the bodies were discovered, Camps was summoned immediately. He was a self-taught pathologist: originally a GP who ran a little laboratory to test blood sugar for diabetics. Then he saw a couple of post-mortems, and concluded that he could do that himself. "Dear Francis bluffed his way through pathology," says Bill Hunt, adding generously, "he actually did some very good things."

In part these good things came from Camps's awareness that he was feeling his way in what was for him new territory. This made him unusually willing to look for outside assistance from different specializations, which, in turn, pushed back the frontiers of forensic pathology. In Rillington Place there was a need to establish how long the bodies had been in the cupboard. The outermost one had bruises around her neck, showing that she had been strangled. Mould was starting to grow from her nostrils, and semen had leaked from her vagina. The other two bodies had pieces of old cloth stuffed between their legs: to absorb any semen, it was assumed. The innermost body was so encrusted with mould that it was impossible to detect whether she, too, had been strangled. Camps took samples and sent Hunt to Kew Gardens to find out whether there was anything peculiar about the mould and what the estimated growth periods might be. In the event it proved to be exactly what biologists would expect to find in a damp London cupboard, and the information about the times the three corpses had been there was not essential once Christie had been caught and made his confessions.

But two other aspects of Camps's work affected Christie's confessions considerably. Christie was a contemptible specimen of humanity: one of the doctors who examined him in prison remarked that he was "full of snivelling hypocrisy". He said whatever he thought would win the approval (or incur the least disapproval) from the people he was talking to. So, although he gave callous and jocular accounts of his monstrous actions when selling his life to the *Sunday Pictorial*, speaking blithely of keeping "a strangling rope" and suggesting that cups of tea played the sort of part in his murders that whisky might in other people's, he was much more circumspect in admitting responsibility for the bodies in his flat when he first made a statement to the police.

He acknowledged he had killed the three women in the alcove (prostitutes named Rita Nelson, Kathleen Maloney and Hectorina MacLennan) as well as a fourth, older woman, whom the police found under his sitting-room floorboards. She was his wife, Ethel Christie, whom he had killed the previous December. He claimed to have strangled her as a mercy killing when he realized that the stress of having to share her house with black people had led her to attempt suicide by taking an overdose of phenobarbitone tablets. Unfortunately for him, his and Ethel's prescribed capsules had survived, and no such overdose had been taken. With only the word of the habitual liar Christie to go on, we just don't know why he killed Ethel. But it is possible that she suspected one of his earlier murders and he no longer trusted her to remain silent; it is also possible that he wanted to return to his squalid and appalling sexual practices, but she was in the way.

His initial explanations of the deaths of the three women in the alcove had a curious and unconvincing similarity about them. Each woman had made unwanted advances, forced herself into his house, even attacked him. Poor Christie felt he "must have gone haywire", for he somehow strangled them. The last one, Miss MacLennan, had caused her own death by somehow catching her clothing on something as she fought him, fatally choking herself.

Professor Camps's findings proved rather a different tale. All the bodies in the alcove had a pinkish tinge. This is a sign of carbon-monoxide poisoning: gassing with fumes from a car exhaust, or the coal gas used in domestic households before the discovery of the North Sea fields. Chemical tests confirmed the presence of carbon monoxide in the bodies. Christie's original confessions said nothing about gas.

Another discovery Camps made was semen in the vaginas of all the women in the alcove; quite an unusually large quantity in one of them. He was fascinated to discover that spermatozoa could still be seen under the microscope, for at that date it was not known that their presence would remain detectable for any length of time if preserved in a dead body. But the innermost body had clearly been hidden for some weeks, and the spermatozoa were still evident. Some commentators still suggest that the cloths (rags or old vests) found tucked in between two of the girls' legs had been put there to absorb or retain the semen. But there was a similar diaper between the legs of Mrs Christie's body in the sitting room, and that body contained no semen. By Christie's account, which we may for once believe, there had been no sexual contact between the two of them for at least two years. So some other explanation is required for Christie's "signature" practice of diapering his victims.

The well-preserved spermatozoa and the observation that a pinkish tinge was visible in the teeth of the women contributed much to Camps's interesting technical booklet *Medical and Scientific Investigations in the Christie Case*. Today it is known that pinkish teeth are not uncommon in corpses: they are found in a fair proportion of drowned bodies, for example, and don't mean very much. But at the time the pinkish teeth contributed to the vital legal question about Christie: had he committed two murders over and above the six demonstrated by the four bodies in his house and two skeletons discovered in his garden within the next few days?

The presence of buried bodies outside was suspected when somebody realized that a "stick" propping up a piece of trellis in the 20 square feet of untidy waste ground was actually a human femur. The garden was then subjected to a more rigorous search than had been applied to Haigh's workshop yard in Crawley. It was marked out into squares with pegs and strings, and the position of the fragments discovered was carefully charted. Today the main advance on this method of detailed searching and recording is the "fingertip search", which requires an officer to comb through the entirety of a small square with his hands before digging down.

Ultimately the nearly complete skeletons of two women were recovered, though the skull of one was missing. Christie later admitted that his dog Judy had unearthed it in 1949, and he threw it into a bombed-out building in St Mark's Road, round the corner. When some children found it a few days later, the coroner assumed it must be the remains of somebody killed by the bomb that destroyed the house.

The two women in the garden were, Christie confessed, his earliest victims. The first, Ruth Fuerst, was a young Austrian who had come to England before the war to train as a nurse, and stayed on, working in a munitions factory. And to supplement her wages she went on the streets at night. Christie was a War Reserve Constable at the time: one of the twenty thousand Special Policemen recruited for the duration. He won two commendations for bringing criminals to justice. He also earned a reputation with some people as a snooping bossyboots who enjoyed petty authority. He was at one with several other serial killers in feeling at home in a job which gave him a uniform and the structured discipline of an authoritarian institution. Indeed, he had been an assistant scoutmaster as a young man, and the most successful period of his life was as a soldier in the First World War. It was probably a personal tragedy that the slight disability left by his being gassed in the trenches led to his being refused by the armed services when he tried to join up again after the war. At that point he slipped into a life of petty crime.

It seems certain that as a War Reserve Constable he enjoyed the opportunity to go legitimately into the sleazy cafés and bars used by prostitutes and force his company on them. He never gave consistent accounts of any of his murders, always improving any story to fit the audience if he had the chance of retelling it. So we cannot be sure of any of the uncorroborated details he gave. But it seems that he had met Ruth Fuerst several times before he killed her, and most likely enjoyed her sexual services. What led him to strangle her while making love in August 1943 will never be known. Certainly he had taken her back to Rillington Place for the occasion, while his wife Ethel was visiting her family in Yorkshire. His claim that Ruth suddenly demanded that he go away with her, and this outraged him, may be dismissed. It is more likely that she affronted him in some way; perhaps by jeering at his manhood, as had happened on his first, adolescent failure to lose his virginity.

Evidently, strangling her while they made love both thrilled and disgusted him. It thrilled him, because it became an experience he repeated at least four times. It disgusted him because, as he said, "While I was having intercourse with her, I strangled her with a piece of rope. I remember urine and excreta coming away from her." This was a strong memory: a precise detail he recalled 10 years later. And it probably explains the diapering. Christie was not interested in mopping up semen. He diapered his wife, whom he certainly did not ravish as he killed her. He wanted the thrill of enjoying sexual satisfaction with an inert, maybe dead or dying woman. But he did not want to face the evacuation which may result from strangulation. For Christie was both filthy and fastidious. His bed was bug-ridden. But he always wore a suit and a collar and tie, and a hat if he was out on the streets. His flat stank. But as a boy he was an excessive hand-washer, like the genuinely fastidious John Haigh. He said that he disapproved of pubs and thought masturbation was disgusting. But he went to pubs to pick up prostitutes, whom he also thought disgusting. And he masturbated to the extent that semen was found soaked into the plimsolls in which he crept around the house. His ideal of himself was as a prissy, lace-curtained prude, and he had so little self-knowledge that he genuinely deplored the psychologist who examined him and was not disgusted by Christie's own sexual actions. And so he could kill a woman; need her inert for his own sexual satisfaction; but need, too, to shield himself from the natural consequences of his actions. Excretion was disgusting. His own repulsive deeds could be pushed out of his mind.

It is probable that his second victim was the first he diapered and the first he gassed. This was Miss Muriel Eady, a co-worker with Christie at the Ultra Radio Works in Acton, where he was employed as a dispatch clerk after resigning from the War Reserve Police. The reason for his resignation following the murder of Ruth Fuerst is not known, but he probably found it embarrassing to continue working in the proximity of a married woman, employed at Harrow Road (where he was stationed), whose husband had learned of Christie's illicit liaison with her and given him a beating shortly before the murder.

He did not have a liaison with Miss Eady. She was a respectable spinster in her thirties with a serious suitor. The couple became friendly with the Christies and occasionally went to the cinema with them. Christie cunningly saw how she might become a victim of his new-found lust for unconscious women when she complained of chronic catarrh. Now, Christie's father had sometimes been nicknamed "the doctor" for his Victorian skill at prescribing simple household remedies for common ailments. Though Ernest Christie's coldness and habit of thrashing his children undoubtedly contributed to Reg's frightful psychological problems, his dictatorial and authoritarian example was one Reg consciously admired, and filial imitation may have encouraged him to make a boast of his own medical skills. He had, in fact, received certificates for his First Aid training with the St John Ambulance Brigade.

It was, however, a barefaced lie when he told Miss Eady he had a special inhalant for her catarrh which he could administer at Rillington Place. What he had prepared was a square jar with a screw top. The jar contained Friar's Balsam, a strong-smelling popular remedy that Miss Eady must have tried already. The lid had two holes bored in it with pieces of rubber tubing passed through them. There was a short one which Miss Eady was to use to inhale the Balsam. And there was a long one which passed over the back of her chair so that she could not see that it was connected to a gas tap. A refinement which Christie may have introduced later was to seal the tube with a bulldog clip, so that he could release gas to bubble into the Balsam without having to go across the room to turn the tap on. The Balsam masked the smell of the gas. The gas made Miss Eady pass out. And Christie was able to strip off her knickers and rape her unconscious body.

His confessions never answered all the questions about his murders. It is unclear to this day how he avoided inhaling enough gas to make himself pass out, given the free flow he was allowing through the jar. Possibly he found some way of taking up a position with his head by an open window. Nor is it clear whether he strangled his victims before, during or after intercourse. His "snivelling hypocritical" prudishness never allowed him to be specific about his brutal and lecherous actions. So some debate has arisen as to whether he should properly be called a necrophile – a pervert driven to copulate with corpses – or whether he was satisfied with having unconscious victims and his murders were just the result of the rapist's determination to eliminate the victim as a witness. Sir Ludovic Kennedy's classic study of the case, so widely accepted as to be known as the "Authorized Version", takes it for granted that Christie wanted dead women to satisfy his lust. Roy Hazelwood of the FBI follows a strict interpretation of necrophilia, saying, "The only classic sign of a necrophile is when you have a dead body and the person is known to have had sex with the dead body. We know, of course, of people who are necrophiliacs who hire prostitutes to pretend to be dead. We know of necrophiliacs who put chloroform over the victim's mouth and cause them to become unconscious so they could pretend that they were dead. It suggests necrophilia, but it's not a classic example of necrophilia."

And on this basis, Hazelwood concludes, "knowing what I know about the case, I'd think it likely that Christie was a necrophile. I believe this is the individual that had the nappies – or as we say in America, the diapers – between the legs of some of the victims, that had seminal stains in them. That would suggest to me that that probably involved necrophilic acts with the victims."

This suggests the probability that Christie gassed his victims into a state of unconsciousness, ravished them and then diapered them so as to avoid the soiling that disgusted him when he strangled them.

Robert Ressler allows a looser definition that would permit such actions to be called necrophilic. "If in fact the person is drugged into a stupor beyond any form of consciousness," he says, "I would say, in my book, if that's what they have to do to obtain a situation where they can have sex with the victim, that would be a necrophile." And in observations that have considerable bearing on

Christie's ultimate defence of insanity, he goes on, "sexual activities … with an inanimate partner or a dead partner certainly indicate a very strong pathology that is based on sexual misfunctioning. A person that can't function with a living human being is obviously a pathologically damaged person."

That view is common sense, and when Christie was tried for the murder of his wife, his counsel, Sir Henry Curtis Bennett, voluntarily put all his other murders in as evidence, and invited the jury to use their common sense and find that a man who gassed, ravished and strangled three women, and stuffed their bodies into a little alcove which he then papered over before walking out of his flat and leaving them for anyone to find, was "mad as a hatter". But the law was bound by the Victorian "MacNaughton Rules", and would only substitute incarceration in an asylum for the prescribed penalty if a criminal could prove that mental defect or disease prevented him from knowing the nature of his actions, or, if he knew this, of knowing that they were wrong. Under this code Christie had no chance. The very omissions in his confessions showed that he knew it was wrong to gas and rape women. His successful attempts to deceive Ethel's relatives into thinking she was still alive and at home over Christmas were a further example of his knowing the nature and quality of his actions. And Sir Henry's argument that Christie was only mad when actually performing his murders was far too subtle for the common sense to which he was appealing.

Executing Christie could not be expected to deter anyone else minded to commit such extraordinary crimes, was not needed to prevent vengeful relatives of his victims from taking the law into their own hands and was not the sort of retribution a just God might be expected to demand, since common sense really did say Christie was too different from normal men to come under normal rules of retributive justice. He did not fit any of the sensible categories under which capital punishment may be justified, and the judge who sentenced him was seen to be in tears as he did so. If it was dreadful that such a horrible specimen of humanity lived, it was somehow even more dreadful to commit him to a squalid ritualized death. But that, of course, was not the reason why John Reginald Halliday Christie did more than any other single person to ensure the abolition of the death penalty in England. While it is extremely unlikely that the two men collaborated in any single murder (although this has been suggested), Christie will always be remembered in association with Timothy Evans, and the address of the house they both occupied will always live in the annals of crime.

As soon as crime reporters heard that bodies had been found in 10 Rillington Place, they saw that an almighty scandal was brewing, over and above the multiple murders now revealed. For in November 1949 a man had been hanged after two strangled bodies were found hidden in the tiny outside wash-house of number 10: 20-year-old Mrs Beryl Evans from the top-floor flat and her 18-month-old daughter, Jeraldine. (Hardly any commentators either notice or respect the Evans's practice of spelling their daughter's name with a "J".)

The case had aroused very little stir in either the Press or the street at the time. It seemed completely open-and-shut. Mrs Evans's husband, Timothy, staying with his aunt and uncle in Wales for a couple of weeks, had suddenly shown up at Merthyr Vale police station and made the unsolicited confession that he had "disposed of" his wife down the drain outside 10 Rillington Place. After being cautioned, he made a statement alleging that an unknown man in a transport café had given him an abortifacient in exchange for a cigarette. His pregnant wife had found it and taken it without his knowledge, and he had come home to find her dead. Fearing this would get him into trouble, he had put her body down the drain.

The Merthyr police telegraphed this improbable information to London, where it was found that the manhole cover over the drain could be unlocked only with a special tool kept by the Water Board, and it was so heavy it took three policemen to lift it. The interior was an inspection pit, and there was no body there and never had been. When this was reported to Evans, he could only say, "Well, I put it there." The Merthyr police concluded that his wife had left him and he had gone off his head.

His second statement to them followed a desultory search of the house which had produced nothing substantial. Evans now claimed that his first statement had been intended to protect "a man called Christie". Christie had offered to procure an abortion for Beryl and, against Tim's wishes, she insisted on going ahead with this on Tuesday November 8. When Tim arrived home from work that evening, Christie told him it had gone wrong and showed him Beryl's body. Christie had taken the body down to the temporarily empty flat on the first floor, whose elderly bachelor occupant, Mr Kitchener, was in hospital having cataracts removed. (Evans later admitted he helped move the body.) Christie advised Evans to sell his furniture and leave London, and promised to dispose of Beryl down a drain and arrange for Jeraldine to be fostered for the time being with a childless young couple in Acton. Evans didn't know their name and address, and he wanted a message sent to his mother in Notting Hill asking her to find out from Christie where Jeraldine was.

When this statement led to serious questioning of the Christies and a more thorough search of the house, several things emerged. Christie was not an abortionist and there was no abortionist's equipment in his flat. He said he understood from Evans that Beryl and Jeraldine were in Brighton with her father, and the Christies had agreed to look after Jeraldine's pram and chair and a suitcase of her clothing, together with her ID card and ration book and a pair of Tim's trousers, until they could be collected. In Tim Evans's flat the police found a briefcase which could be identified by a half-erased label as one that had been reported stolen. They also found some newspaper cuttings about the recent notorious murder of Stanley Setty by Donald Hume: a case of rogues falling out until one knifed the other, dismembered his body, parcelled up the bits and dropped them into the English Channel from a private light aeroplane.

And in the wash-house they found Beryl's body, concealed behind some paint pots and pieces of timber, wrapped up in a tablecloth and a blanket under the copper. Behind the door, half concealed by more pieces of timber, was Jeraldine's body. She had been strangled with a tie which was still around her neck.

Scotland Yard immediately sent two officers to Wales to arrest Evans on the holding charge of possessing the stolen briefcase. They were strictly ordered to tell him nothing about the bodies. When Evans was brought back to Ladbroke Grove Police Station, Superintendent Jennings showed him the pile of clothes which had been found on Beryl and Jeraldine, with the tie at the top, and told him that his wife and daughter had been found dead and that he suspected Evans of murdering them. Evans immediately admitted it. He and Beryl had been having ever-increasing rows about her running them into debt, he said, and he had finally lost his temper on the Tuesday evening and strangled her with a piece of rope he had carried up from his van. He hid the body in Mr Kitchener's flat. Two days later, when he came home from work, he strangled Jeraldine and took both bodies down to the wash-house. Then he sold his furniture and left for Wales. The full statement was taken by Inspector Black and Superintendent Jennings (who had conducted the fruitless search of the Gloucester Road basement where Haigh killed the McSwans) and was completed before midnight. Over the next couple of days Evans added details to his confession in scraps of conversation with various officials. He had taken his wife's wedding ring and sold it to a jeweller in Swansea. (The police already knew of this sale, and had not told him.) He had killed Jeraldine, he told Sergeant Trevallian, because he could not stop her crying. His confessions stood uncontradicted until his mother came to visit him in prison and asked him why he did it, and he burst out, "I didn't do it, Mam. Christie did it." And that became his story and his defence, essentially following, unchanged, the lines of the tale of the unsuccessful abortion that he had told in Merthyr Vale. He knew nothing about Jeraldine's death, he said. And he didn't know how the bodies got into the wash-house.

And what did Rillington Place think of this? Pauline Hildreth was 11 or 12 at the time. She thought of Mr and Mrs Evans as a nice couple. She used to get permission to push Jeraldine up and down the street in her pram on sunny days if the baby had been left outside and was crying. And so she felt natural girlish shock: "It was awful … I mean, we couldn't imagine that her husband had done that: we couldn't imagine that – you know, when she was pregnant as well." Evelyn Dymond, grown up by the time of the murders, had a more soberly realistic view. "The street all thought that Evans had done it," she said. "They all thought Evans had done it because the neighbours had heard them rowing. They always kept their window halfway up and they would row a lot, the Evanses." Timothy Evans had a poor reputation in the Rillington Place: "I can remember he used to have other women in as well, and I think they had quite a lot of rows and one thing and another. So I heard from different neighbours. They'd overhear the rows … that he'd taken other women in there."

They did indeed have rows. Mrs Rosina Swan's windows overlooked the Evans's, and on winter evenings she could sometimes see their shadows silhouetted against the blind. Some weeks before the bodies were found she heard one of the recurrent rows and saw the shadow of Evans with his hands murderously gripped round Beryl's throat. The bruises, some weeks old, were still present on Beryl's neck when Dr Donald Teare carried out the post-mortem on her body. But Evans was quite a small man: just 5 feet 6 inches tall and weighing a mere 9½ stone. He was unable to do Beryl lasting damage with his bare hands.

Although Evans claimed that the rows were about his wife's debts and bad housekeeping, they could also be about his spendthrift drinking and his tendency not to give her housekeeping money. Usually his mother, Mrs Thomazine Probert, took Beryl's side, recognizing her son's dishonesty and fecklessness. But she blamed Beryl when the girl started a flirtation with a painter at her workplace, and told Tim. Tim went there and created such a violent scene that Beryl lost her job and was forced to find part-time work at a shop in Oxford Street.

The Evans family all knew about another evening of mad violence that Tim precipitated. He was a persistent and stupid fantasizing liar, telling casual acquaintances absurd tales of having recently been to Egypt, or being the brother of a rich car salesman who was going to give him a posh car. He told calculating, self-interested lies to his family and employers, and in the weeks before Beryl's death he told her that he had been offered a job with the aircraft manufacturers De Havilland which would take him to Bristol. (He was a van driver for a local bakery.) Beryl invited a young friend, Lucy, from the Oxford Street shop to stay with her while Tim was away. But of course there was no De Havilland job and Tim wasn't away. There were difficulties about his having to sleep in the kitchen while Beryl and Lucy shared the bed. There were difficulties when Tim started eyeing up Lucy. They culminated in a screaming row when Mrs Probert came round and hit the young girl. Tim tried to throw Beryl out of the window and stormed off with Lucy to try to stay with the Evans's friends, Charles and Joan Vincent. The Vincents hadn't got room for them, so they spent one night in a bed and breakfast; another in a cheap hotel, where their single night of lovemaking was no great success. Lucy declared that she never wanted to see Tim again – and never did see him or Beryl. Tim threatened to "do her in" by running his van over her. And Beryl took serious thought about getting a divorce. Tim was undoubtedly a violent and rather dangerous little man with a vile temper.

So the street was shocked when he accused Christie of somehow killing Beryl. "They used to think, Well, fancy trying to blame Mr Christie for that!" recalls Mrs Dymond. "I think we all felt sorry for Christie, really, that it should be suggested that he did it."

This was not because of any close friendships the Christies had formed. Ludovic Kennedy was supremely accurate in saying that Christie enjoyed the advantage of being a middle-class man in a working-class neighbourhood. Everybody else enjoyed the intensely warm, close community life in the little cul-de-sac whose brick wall made it a perfect playground for children in those days when there was little traffic on residential streets. On summer evenings people stood outside their doors and gossiped. There were tremendous street parties to celebrate national occasions, and every Guy Fawkes Night the Rillington Place bonfire burned a hole in the tarmac.

The Christies played no part in this. "They were very reserved and they didn't join in," recalls Evelyn Dymond. "I think we got the impression that he was a bit aloof of us, really. But we didn't take no notice. If that was the way he wanted, they just accepted." "A very quiet respectable man that kept himself to himself," remembers Pauline Hildreth. And both women recalled the formal dress that marked out Christie's status: he wore a trilby hat, whereas "their" men wore caps; he wore a collar and tie, which suggested a teacher or a doctor. "And he was always polite, you didn't hear him swear or anything."

Only Evelyn Dymond's uncle disapproved of Christie. A lonely bachelor living in the top-floor flat of number 10 before the Evans, he told his niece that Christie was "a bad man. He digs big holes in the garden late at night." Evelyn disregarded her uncle's prescient suspicion of Christie's nocturnal activities. The misanthropic views of an old solitary weren't taken seriously.

So when Evans had been convicted – as he inevitably was after the confessions he had made – and hanged, which caused no sensation at the time, the street, Press, public and police were all sure justice had been done. Christie won a good deal of sympathy for enduring Evans's false accusation, especially as it produced the embarrassing revelation that he had a criminal record, although he had gone straight for 17 years and served with honour (if quite improperly) as a wartime police constable.

And when bodies turned up following his sole occupancy of the ground-floor flat at number 10, "Well, everybody was, like, gobsmacked then!" says Pauline Hildreth. "Disbelief," said Evelyn Dymond. "You just couldn't believe that he would do – he *could* do that! Anyway, 'It must have been somebody else', sort of thing."

Whatever could or could not be believed about Christie, one thing was immediately apparent. The mere presence of two women, strangled with ligatures and buried in the garden by Christie before Evans even came to live in the road, cast definite "reasonable doubt" on Evans's conviction. Indeed, only the most unreasonable of people could possibly maintain that there was no doubt about whether or not Evans killed his wife. Unfortunately, capital punishment induces intense unreason in both supporters and opponents. And the Home Secretary of the time, Sir David Maxwell Fyfe, was so fatuously committed to capital punishment that he had given fortune the hostage of declaring that no innocent man ever had been or ever could be executed under British justice. He had the strongest of causes for upholding the verdict of "Guilty" against Evans.

Yet as part of his unsuccessful plea of insanity, Christie now admitted to killing Beryl Evans: not, indeed, as part of a pre-planned pseudo-abortion as Evans's confession intimated, but in an attempt to help her complete the suicide he found her attempting in front of her own gas fire, and in return for an offer of sex which he found himself unable to accomplish.

More sophisticated observers than the Rillington Place folk went back to the records and found all sorts of inconsistencies and problems in the evidence presented at Evans's trial. Questions were asked in Parliament. Evans's mother and sisters pushed for a hearing to grant him a free pardon. So before Christie could be executed, Maxwell Fyfe appointed John Scott Henderson QC to hold an inquiry and interview Christie. Scott Henderson looked a reliable safe pair of hands. He was not an establishment hack, but a former NCO who had fought gallantly at Gallipoli and then put himself through university and bar finals after the war. His record on social matters was liberal rather than reactionary. And he had a reputation for mastering complicated and lengthy briefs very rapidly.

With only 11 days to complete his investigation into this case, however, he made a complete bish of it. Despite his own interviews with Christie, and the exhumation of Beryl's body for examination by the joint team of Teare, Camps and Simpson, his report failed to answer so many of the questions raised by protesters that it produced a storm of parliamentary objection and he was compelled to write a supplementary report. This was little better. But Maxwell Fyfe was in a government with a comfortable majority and pushed through its acceptance. Essentially, Scott Henderson's case was that Evans had spontaneously confessed and only withdrew his confessions when he saw the gallows looming. Christie had never confessed to Jeraldine's murder, and had had no apparent motive to kill her. He had been encouraged to confess to Beryl's by his defence. The higher the number of victims, the greater the appearance of insanity, ran the argument. Or, as Christie crudely put it to the prison chaplain, "The more the merrier." His confession was not supported by the pathologists' report on the exhumed body, which detected no signs of carbon-monoxide poisoning. And Christie had withdrawn his confession subsequently, and declined to repeat it to Scott Henderson.

This confident weighing of the words of two habitual liars did not silence the pro-Evans lobby. Books and pamphlets continued to appear giving detailed accounts of the case, culminating in Ludovic Kennedy's magisterial *10 Rillington Place*. This exculpated Evans on the following grounds:

1. Evans was not a violent man. His marriage was basically happy, despite the tensions provoked by poverty and crowded conditions. He adored Jeraldine and never offered any reason for killing her.

2. As an ineducable illiterate with an IQ of 65 – a "high-grade mental defective" in the view of one doctor who examined him – Evans was putty in the hands of Christie, an intelligent man with an IQ of 129 – quite capable of university education had he been properly directed.

3. Evans's detailed statement accusing Christie was the truth as he understood it. Christie had pretended to offer an abortion for Beryl, who had insisted on going ahead with it. (Of course, this was vitiated by the evidence that Christie could not have been an abortionist.)

4. The police probably planted the stolen briefcase and newspaper cuttings on Hume and Setty in Evans's room to give an excuse for a holding charge and some evidence that he was interested in murder. Evans had no record of dishonesty, and was illiterate

and so could not have read the cuttings.

5. Superintendent Jennings and Inspector Black had "brainwashed" Evans by questioning him until the small hours of the morning, dropping details of the ways the bodies were hidden to make sure his confession was convincing. Then they pretended to have taken an unprompted statement that was completed before midnight.

6. At the time of the Evans murders, workmen were in and out of 10 Rillington Place making repairs. They replastered the ceiling of the wash-house where the bodies were found and kept their tools there until Friday November 11, on which day the plasterer's mate swept and cleared it, and there were definitely no bodies there. Yet Evans said he killed Beryl on the 8th and Jeraldine on the 10th, and took the bodies to the wash-house that evening.

7. The police recalled the workmen and kept them waiting around until they made them change their statements to say that the wash-house was cleared on November 10, and they would not have noticed thereafter any bodies hidden behind pieces of timber.

8. Dr Teare's original post-mortem on Beryl contained evidence of post-mortem sexual intercourse, and if he had bothered to take swabs he would surely have found semen: evidence that she was a victim of the necrophile Christie.

9. Dr Camps believed he saw pinkish teeth when Beryl's body was exhumed, confirming the presence of carbon monoxide.

10. Christie had collected four locks of women's pubic hairs in a tobacco tin. One of these matched Beryl's hair, and, indeed, in one of his statements Christie had said it came from her.

That, today, is popularly believed to be the truth about the case, and its accusations against the police lie at the heart of much subsequent popular suspicion of police interrogation methods. The book's success encouraged Home Secretary Roy Jenkins to appoint Sir Daniel Brabin to re-examine the affair in 1966. Brabin's first conclusion was that whatever anyone made of the evidence, there was inevitably reasonable doubt about Evans's guilt. This was the first piece of common-sense honesty from an establishment figure invited to comment officially. It gave Jenkins the opportunity to grant Evans a posthumous "free pardon" – the only way to reverse a guilty verdict in English law.

But Brabin's further conclusions flabbergasted Kennedy and other pro-Evans campaigners. For after studying more evidence than anyone had hitherto seen, Brabin concluded that Evans probably did kill Beryl, but Christie probably killed Jeraldine. Brabin admitted that it was impossible to be certain about the truth, given that both men were habitual liars and each had both confessed and denied committing the two murders.

It was news to the campaigners that Christie had ever admitted to murdering Jeraldine, but it was there among the statements. After his conviction, while awaiting the medical report on his fitness to be hanged, Christie had said to hospital attendant J.A. Roberts, "If the police only knew that they could charge me with the murder of the Evans's baby girl ... but they can't do anything about it now." Like Evans's confession to Sergeant Trevallian that he had a reason for killing Jeraldine, adequate to his feeble mentality, this was never part of the Authorized Version.

Brabin proved that Evans was violent and quite capable of seriously assaulting his wife. It was clear that his family had believed that this black sheep committed the murders at the time he was executed, and then, when Christie's exposure showed them they must have been wrong, they naturally rushed to the other extreme and sanctified the memory of a son and brother who had really been a grave problem. And their perfectly honest misrecollection misled Kennedy.

There was also a statement from the murderer Donald Hume that Evans had confessed to him in prison that he stood by while Christie strangled Jeraldine. Since Evans had an immature, hero-worshipping attitude to Hume and associated with him whenever possible, this was given credence by the writer Rupert Furneaux, who assumed the two were friends. But in fact Hume deeply resented Evans, who he believed had shopped him to the authorities for a minor infringement of prison rules. Besides, Hume was another notorious liar: he succeeded in lying his way out of his own murder charge, and only confessed the truth after he had served a sentence for disposing of the body. However, despite Brabin, who accepted Evans's guilt, nobody has ever persuasively challenged the evidence of Evans's aunt and uncle in Wales, who found him evasive and unconvincing in his accounts of Beryl's whereabouts but obviously certain that Jeraldine was alive and well and a continuing joy to him.

When the papers on the case were opened to the public in 1994, certain corrections to the Authorized Version were immediately apparent. It was absolutely confirmed that Evans was a violent, dishonest and unpleasant man, constantly trying to secure money to which he wasn't entitled, losing his temper when crossed and physically attacking Beryl. John Hurt's virtuoso performance in Richard Fleischer's film *Ten Rillington Place*, portraying a harmless halfwit unable to comprehend how desperately trying to tell the truth for once was inexorably leading him to the noose, was a perfect recreation of Kennedy's characterization. But the harmlessness meant that it wasn't Evans.

The police were clearly exonerated from most of the campaigners' charges. The stolen briefcase had been pinched from a research student whose room faced the flat of the Evans's friends Charles and Joan Vincent. By Evans's own admission, the Vincents had brought the briefcase and a stolen blanket to him and Beryl because they could not dispose of them. Evans sold the blanket to Lucy for her mother, and had not yet found a buyer for the briefcase. The Vincents denied this story, and despite the briefcase and blanket's having been reported stolen from a room to which they had access, the police decided not to proceed against them. But there was no question that the police had not planted anything to incriminate Evans and enable a holding charge.

Jennings's notebook has survived, and shows that he had made a first draft and a fair copy of Evans's statement, and Evans himself signed and dated it correctly. It fits the times the police ascribed to the interview. The campaigners had been confused by a newspaper report that a man was "being questioned by police" in the small hours of the morning. This was a misleading interpretation of the Scotland Yard release that a man was "helping police with their enquiries" – a formulation covering being held on remand and sleeping in a cell.

Nor had the workmen been badgered into altering times to suit police theories about the bodies going into the wash-house before it was cleared on Friday. The facing wall made the wash-house so dark that even in clear daylight the police needed a torch to see inside it. They were content that the workmen might have missed the bodies as long as they weren't placed there before the men finished plastering the roof. But the plasterer's mate was a 68-year-old gentleman with a dreadful short-term memory. He placed Evans in Rillington Place during working hours on Thursday November 10, a day when Evans was quite definitely making deliveries in Brighton with the salesman who always accompanied him. Evans did not arrive home until the evening, at which time, according to his confession, he strangled Beryl. It was to correct this point that the police were most anxious to see the workmen, and they didn't even notice that the revised statement, placing Evans in the house a day earlier, still left serious conflict in the old man's confused recollections. For he said he saw Evans about the place on two consecutive days, on one of which he came downstairs and jumped over the hole in the hallway where the flooring was being repaired. And that work didn't start until Friday November 12.

But what the police missed, defence lawyers were unlikely to pick up. Evans's confessions, starting with the completely unprompted appearance saying he had "disposed of" his wife, really meant that establishing a precise order of events was painting the lily.

As for the medical evidence, Dr Teare was quite certain that there had been no pink coloration of Beryl's body at the time of her original post-mortem. His colleagues agreed that he could not have missed it if she had suffered carbon-monoxide poisoning. Furthermore, if Christie had used gas on her in the way he claimed, it was impossible to see how he could have failed to pass out himself.

The pubic hairs in the tin could not be Beryl's. They were cut at both ends, indicating that the woman in question had given herself something along the lines of a bikini trim. There was no sign of Beryl's having done any such thing in the weeks prior to her death.

And Dr Teare had categorically not suggested any post-mortem intercourse. He had seen bruising in the vagina which was most likely to have been caused by Beryl's syringing herself in an attempt to force a miscarriage. He had examined her carefully with a magnifying glass, and was positive that there was no deposit of semen. Again, his colleagues agreed that he would have got this right. He did observe fresh bruises on Beryl's knee and inner thigh, which suggested that somebody had tried to force her legs open. This actually matched Christie's claim that he tried to have intercourse with her, but could not manage it. It did not support the suggestion made later that Evans had attempted marital rape some hours or days earlier.

All this led the first person to examine the papers to write a book claiming that Evans had murdered both Beryl and Jeraldine. The author, John Eddowes, was the son of a solicitor who had been one of the leading pro-Evans campaigners. John Eddowes knew that his father, Michael, had died in a mental hospital as a paranoid schizophrenic. And following his success in the Evans case, Michael Eddowes had become a Kennedy buff and persuaded others to share his delusion that the Lee Harvey Oswald shot by Jack Ruby was a Russian mole smuggled into the place of the real Oswald. Exhuming Oswald's body proved this to be rubbish, and John Eddowes feared that his father had similarly misled the public over Evans and Christie. But his reconstruction of the case was forced to lean heavily on the original inaccurate memories of the plasterer's mate. Skipping over Evans's definite presence in Brighton all day (except to say that it was probably to look for a place to throw the bodies in the sea) and totally obscuring the accompanying presence of the salesman, Mr Williams, John Eddowes had Tim slipping back to Rillington Place during Thursday November 10. He relied totally on the workman's shaky memory to uphold the idea of a "mystery woman" who supposedly went out for the afternoon with Beryl and the baby on the Tuesday when Evans claimed Christie killed his wife. Despite some veiling, it is evident that Eddowes's "mystery woman" is Evans's sister, Maureen, and he is accusing her and Evans's other relations of deliberately concealing their certain knowledge that Beryl was alive when Tim said Christie killed her, and that Evans himself must have killed her. This matches absolutely nobody's impression of the Evanses and Proberts.

And to explain the presence of Jeraldine's body in the washhouse without implicating Christie, Eddowes has to postulate a totally hypothetical and completely unconvincing yarn about Evans carrying the child's body to Wales and back in his suitcase. His noble attempt to prevent the public from being misled by his mentally disturbed father was given serious consideration by Richard Whittington-Egan, the doyen of true-crime writers, and convinced Colin Wilson, who had already accepted Hume's story. But neither writer had seen the Metropolitan Police papers or studied the full Brabin and Henderson reports. While its details may be wrong, the general outline of Kennedy's Authorized Version, which blames Christie for both murders, carries complete conviction. There is even good evidence on the files that the police themselves had suspected the presence of an abortionist in Rillington Place, and set a watch on number 10 before the bodies were discovered. This strongly supports Kennedy's speculation that Christie used the pretence of medical skills to try to lure women with unwanted pregnancies into his lair.

Sir Ludovic quite properly forced changes in Eddowes's book, whose first edition libelled him by suggesting that his work was negligent and dishonest. And the sensational nature of Christie's crimes coloured the popular view of the sexual multiple murderer for the next decade.

1953–1965

CHRISTIE WAS A MEAGRE, middle-aged man, an ordinary clerical worker and a sexual inadequate. Since his best-known predecessor, Peter Kürten, the Düsseldorf monster, was another neatly suited, middle-aged clerical worker with a dowdy wife who never found him sexually demanding, this was thought to be the model of the multiple sex killer. It was not realized that Kürten had got away with killing since he was very young, and Christie was unusual in taking up sex murder at the late age of 44. When the young, reasonably good-looking and extravagantly sexually active Albert DeSalvo was identified by Massachusetts police as the Boston Strangler in 1965, it came as something of a surprise to the general public.

Yet a mere five years after Christie, a Scottish court tried a good-looking young man who had perpetrated eight or possibly nine murders on four or possibly five separate occasions. Peter Manuel, however, was a professional thief, who killed six of his victims in the course of two robberies. He was not identified as first and foremost a serial killer. He was seen as a plain crook, whose nasty habits included rape and indecent assault, and who completed some of his crimes by killing the victims.

In the summer of 1956 Manuel shot dead Mrs Marion Watt, her sister Margaret Brown and Mrs Brown's daughter, Vivienne, after breaking into their house south of Glasgow while Mr Watt was away on a fishing trip. He was not suspected. The police thought Mr Watt had driven back overnight to murder his wife. Manuel then did one of the serial killer's occasional peculiar actions: he injected himself into the case unnecessarily. He was arrested for burglary and happened to be in Barlinnie Prison while Mr Watt was held there. He told Mr Watt's solicitor that he had information about the murders which could clear his client. Although his account persuaded both Mr Watt and the solicitor that he must have been either the perpetrator or an accomplice, he was not charged. But Mr Watt was released.

This was actually Manuel's second murderous outing. In January 1956 he had taken 17-year-old Anne Kneilands into woodland near Glasgow and battered her to death. He had been questioned as someone in the neighbourhood at the time, but was never suspected.

The authorities were later sure that in December 1957, after he had come out of jail, Manuel went to England and shot Newcastle taxi driver Stanley Dunn. But charges were never brought. Manuel was to be tried under Scottish jurisdiction for his eight Scottish murders.

His fifth came soon after Stanley Dunn's death. Like Anne Kneilands' killing, this murder was also motivated by sex. Seventeen-year-old Isabelle Cooke was killed and buried in a field between Glasgow and the town of Uddingston, where she was going to meet her boyfriend for a dance. Her petticoat and knickers were found, but her body was not traced until Manuel was arrested and questioned a month later.

Manuel was arrested for another mass murder in an Uddingston family home he was robbing. He shot Mr and Mrs Peter Smart and their 10-year-old son. He was trapped, however, by a line of enquiry that would be refined in the hunt for the Yorkshire Ripper 20 years later. He was seen to be spending more money than usual, and the police secured a new £5 note he had passed. It was traced back to the issuing bank, and found to have been given to Mr Smart when he drew cash for a holiday. Manuel was arrested, and confessed to all his murders.

Like the later young and good-looking serial killer Ted Bundy in America, Manuel distinguished himself by taking over his own defence from his lawyers and winning compliments from the judge on his competence. Not that his defence had any chance of success. He claimed that the police had extracted his confession by force. He was convicted on all counts except the murder of Anne Kneilands, and hanged at Barlinnie.

With the majority of his killings and three out of five murderous outings supporting robberies, Manuel looks superficially like a man who simply went too far in his criminal life. He doesn't evince either the sort of compulsion that drove a Ripper or a Christie, or any professional need to encompass death as part of a criminal MO like Smith and Haigh. But it is no longer felt that the sexual serial killer is essentially driven by erotic desire. John Douglas's conclusions are drawn, as he has said, not from his own insightful creative deductions, but from what a sufficient number of criminals have themselves told him, so that he could compare their claims with the facts of their situation until the weight of numbers indicated that he was hearing the truth. And he found that the "violent predatory criminal" – a perfect categorization of Manuel – suffers "a severe lack of self-worth and self-confidence", with most convicted sexual predators showing markedly higher intelligence than the generality of the prison population. As a result of dysfunctional or abusive parenting they have "a strong feeling of inadequacy, of not being able to measure up", which wars with "a feeling of superiority, grandiosity; societal mores were not meant for them". And so what comes to motivate many, if not most, of them is "a desire for power and control that comes from a background where they felt powerless and out of control".

Here, at last, we have a flexible account of the serial killer which factors in many of the features previously suggested from the scholar's desk, but without the mechanical replicability of Joel Norris's theory concerning damage to the limbic region of the brain, or the dependence on subjective social-class evaluation inherent in Elliott Leyton's or Colin Wilson's theories. With Manuel we are certainly looking at a man with a dysfunctional upbringing and a dreadful record of juvenile crime. We have a manipulative narcissist who insists on conducting his own defence, and has the intelligence to make a good job of it. But nobody has suggested that Manuel was a misguided class warrior, or the victim of a head injury.

The age of murder's innocence had still a handful of years to run. But more vicious activities were in the air. In 1963 Boston became the first major city in the twentieth century to experience mass panic fear of a roving sex maniac. Between 1962 and 1964 the Boston Strangler gained access to the apartments of 12 single women, raped and mutilated them, then strangled them with a ligature tied in a pretty, mocking bow. Before his ravages ceased, London was hearing about "Jack the Stripper", the killer who left "Nudes in the Thames". Actually more of them were found beside the Thames than in it, and four of his seven victims were dumped in side streets and back alleys. Since all were prostitutes, however, the public was not really terrified or outraged. With a trace of embarrassment in this age of political correctness, Mrs Evelyn Dymond recalls that back in the 1950s Christie never seemed as bad as Haigh, because, "The women that Christie murdered were prostitutes, anyway. So we thought the worse of them for that, I suppose. But none the more for that they all belonged to somebody."

The Stripper's victims all belonged to somebody, too, and the police, directed by Detective Superintendent "Big John" Du Rose, made a tremendous effort to catch him. Police roadblocks stopped traffic on the west London streets after midnight and demanded explanations from men who were out driving at that time. Policewomen disguised themselves as prostitutes, looking out for kerb-crawling punters who wanted "blow jobs". (A similarly disguised policewoman had helped break up a cocaine ring run by Piccadilly street girls as early as 1921.) The forensic laboratories studied flecks of paint found on some of the dead women, and concluded that the bodies had been kept in a cool, cement-floored room close to a garage that sprayed cars. And when one of three final suspects committed suicide and the murders stopped, the police were sure they knew who the Stripper had been. He was a security guard employed at the north-west London industrial estate where the garage that temporarily stored the bodies was located.

Nineteen sixty-six was a turn-around year. The death penalty in Britain had been abolished the year before. As if to confirm the worst fears of those policemen who believed this put their lives at risk, three absurdly panicky petty thieves shot and killed three unarmed plain-clothes police officers in a quiet residential street near Wormwood Scrubs Prison in outer London. In America, mass murder hit the headlines, as Richard Speck killed and raped eight nurses in a Chicago hostel, while Charles Whitman gunned down 21 innocent passers-by from a tower at the University of Texas and went on shooting until police officers managed to break in and shoot him dead.

But it was the murders exposed in England within months of the gallows being chopped down that did most to fuel anti-abolitionists' rage. And for 35 years Myra Hindley would be the tabloid press's ideal incarnation of evil: the British sensational journalist's equivalent of America's Charles Manson.

THE MOORS
MURDERS

ON OCTOBER 7, 1965 a dawn telephone call aroused the little police station in Hyde, Cheshire. This township of 35,000 souls has now been absorbed into Greater Manchester, and was already absorbing overspill population from the huge conurbation. The call came from a public phone box, where 17-year-old David Smith and his 19-year-old wife, Maureen, were cowering, armed with a hammer and screwdriver for self-protection. When they were taken to the police station, Smith described the horrific murder he had witnessed the previous night. Maureen's sister, Myra Hindley, had asked Smith to her grandmother's house, where Myra lived with her boyfriend, Ian Brady. The pretext was to collect some miniature wine bottles. While Smith was looking at them in the kitchen, Hindley suddenly screamed to him to go and "Help Ian!" In the sitting room, Brady was standing over 17-year-old Edward Evans, who sat on the sofa. As Smith came in Brady smashed down an axe on Evans's head, splitting it. He hit Evans again as he lay moaning on the floor and then strangled him with electric-light flex. Then he handed Smith the axe, saying, "Feel the weight of it", and when Hindley came in, he remarked coolly that this had been "the messiest one yet".

Smith, fearing all the time that he would be axed next, helped Hindley and Brady clean up. He was astonished by their coolness; astonished that Hindley simply made cups of tea for refreshment, and that neither was concerned about Mrs Maybury, Hindley's grandmother, sleeping upstairs.

David Smith was not a young man of good character. He had convictions for theft and assault, and he admitted that his association with Brady included plans to rob a bank. But his story was never doubted for a moment. His genuine terror ensured that even the parts that were not first-hand eyewitness material carried credence. He said Hindley and Brady had committed other murders. He was believed. He said they kept guns in the house. He was believed. Superintendent Bob Talbot, Chief Inspector Bob Wills, Detective Sergeant Alex Carr and Detective Constable Ian Fairley of Cheshire CID went to 16 Wardle Brook Avenue on the Hattersley overspill estate. Fairley, looking back 35 years, is astonished by the way they arrested a potentially armed murderer in the age of innocence. "No policeman was armed, there was no armed response teams, there was no firearms people. As far as the police were concerned, we just went there and went in the house. We had no idea whether we were going to be confronted by anybody with a gun, but we had a job to do and we went there."

Police patrol cars parked at various points around the estate showed that Hattersley was effectively sealed off against Brady's escaping. Superintendent Talbot made a famous impromptu use of disguise when he realized that number 16 Wardle Brook Avenue could be reached only from a completely exposed walkway, leaving a police officer vulnerable to gunshots from the front room. So he borrowed a white coat and a basket from a baker's rounds-man working the street, and surprised Myra Hindley when she opened the door to him.

She was significantly less surprised that the police were visiting than that an unordered bread delivery should be made. She coldly denied the presence of any man in the house. But the police officers swept past her and found Brady in his underwear on a sofa bed in the sitting room. And after Hindley made a short pretence of not having the keys to the second bedroom, upstairs, they entered it and found Edward Evans's body trussed up, as well as the guns David Smith had rightly said were in the house. Brady was arrested and taken to the police station, where he coldly and laconically admitted the killing, saying it was just an argument that got out of hand, and trying to throw as much blame as possible on to Smith.

At this point the police might easily have brought their investigation to a close. A murder had been reported. The murderer had confessed. He was trying to cast the blame on a criminal associate. There was no need to pay any attention to that associate's unsubstantiated claim that there were other murders which he hadn't witnessed and hadn't believed in until he saw Edward Evans butchered. After a productive week, Chief Superintendent Benfield of Cheshire CID was quite keen to send Brady for trial and bring the case to an end. But Smith insisted that there were bodies buried on the moors and that there was written and photographic evidence of this in 16 Wardle Brook Avenue, together with sadistic and fascist literature.

The last point was completely untrue. The police had searched the house thoroughly. There were small blood splashes from Evans's murder that had escaped the general clean-up. There was a number of photographs of empty moorland landscapes. There was just one thing supporting Smith's accusations. In Myra Hindley's Mini-Traveller van was a handwritten plan for disposing of Evans's body on the moors. Patricia Hodges, a little girl living next door to Grandma Maybury's house, told the police conducting house-to-house interviews that Hindley and Brady had taken her up to Saddleworth Moor in Hindley's van. But it had been an innocent sort of picnic, where the couple drank a little wine, admired the view and then drove home again.

The police were divided. Some thought Smith should have been arrested with Brady, and that Brady's accusations against him should be investigated. He wasn't doing himself any favours by going on trying to make somebody take him seriously. Former Chief Superintendent Ian Fairley pays this young petty criminal a well-deserved compliment when he says, "I've got to say how many mums and dads today, or how many children who are adults today in that area, can thank Dave Smith they're still here because he had enough guts, determination that he wasn't going to sit back and see somebody killed the way he did, and he told us about it."

Smith was the first of four men who did more than anyone else to bring Brady and Hindley to justice. The second was Detective Sergeant Alex Carr, whose police instincts to believe him were right on target; who bore with ridicule from his colleagues and hostility from his superiors as he followed up Smith's vague claims; and who had one absolute brainwave. He asked Smith where Hindley and Brady used to go of an evening in Manchester: which pubs and clubs did they frequent? Smith told him they preferred railway stations and station cafés. And behind Superintendent Benfield's back, Carr telephoned the Manchester Transport Police and had them check station left-luggage offices to see whether any unclaimed baggage was sitting there.

Two days later a famous clue would be found: a left-luggage office ticket hidden in the spine of Hindley's missal. The ticket covered two suitcases which became notorious. But they were already in police hands. The ticket's real function was to link her circumstantially to the physical evidence in the suitcases. They contained the sadistic and fascist literature and pornography Smith had described. They contained photographs and photographic negatives of bleak moorland landscapes. They contained a set of pictures of a little girl on a bed, gagged with an enormous scarf, stripped of her clothing and photographed in pornographic poses. They contained a reel-to-reel audio tape (cassettes were not yet on the market) which would make Hindley the most hated woman in England. And one suitcase contained an exercise book with some names written in it. Most of them proved to be friends of Brady's. But a name which Brady claimed was that of a friend in Hull – a friend who was never traced – was John Kilbride. And that name rang immediate bells with the police.

On November 23, 1963, 12-year-old John Kilbride from Ashton-under-Lyne, another of the suburban townships on the fringe of Greater Manchester, had gone missing. He went out at the end of the afternoon, as he frequently did, to the Ashton street market, where he helped market traders clear away their stalls. For carrying boxes he was rewarded with a few pennies, which he needed to supplement his pocket money to pay for visits to the cinema. He was a friendly, well-behaved child from a textbook "poor but honest" family: mum, dad and seven children packed into a three-bedroom semi. As the eldest child, John shared one of the bedrooms with his brother Danny, who misses him to this day, saying, "There was no badness in him whatsoever. He'd help anybody – the neighbours – anything. He'd literally help anybody and wouldn't accept anything for it. And I know this for a fact, because I've been with him once or twice, and I said, 'Why didn't you take it? You know, we could have gone to the shops or something.' he said, 'No, because they're all heart, they haven't got a lot of money.' That's the kind of lad he was."

Even cynical policemen were soon convinced that John was no mischief-maker to run away and get into trouble. After the usual 24-hour delay in case he'd just wandered off and got lost – a delay deeply resented by all the victims' surviving relatives – the police's missing-person search moved rapidly into high gear. Photographs of John were reproduced and posted on walls, lamp-posts and trees with the question "Have you seen this boy?" Radio appeals were broadcast. Hundreds of helpful and misguided sightings were followed up. But apart from a handful of people who had seen John in the market around five o'clock, there was nothing. And for two years there had been nothing.

Today we know what happened. A lady with dyed blonde hair spotted a child unaccompanied by friends or adults. She asked this boy – the lad who would always help a neighbour in any way he could – whether he would come with her in her van to help her shift some boxes or bags. He agreed. He needn't be home for another hour and a half, and helping people with boxes was exactly what he went to the market for. He went with her in her little van to Saddleworth Moor. And there the lady's boyfriend, a taciturn man with a Scottish accent, sexually assaulted him on Hollin Brow Knoll, strangled him and dug a hole in which he dumped the body upside down.

DS Carr and his team were faintly surprised that they failed to identify the little girl in the photographs as immediately as they spotted John Kilbride's name. In fact it was not until they were watching a television programme on children who had gone missing in the Greater Manchester area over the preceding four years that they recognized 10-year-old Lesley Ann Downey. She had disappeared on Boxing Day 1964, over a year after John. She had gone to a fair with friends, her mother Ann and stepfather Alan West assuming that the friends' parents would be supervising the children. When Lesley Ann did not arrive home, and it transpired that the other children had left the fair without her, the Wests were absolutely appalled. They were even angrier than the Kilbrides about the compulsory delay before an all-out police effort was mounted. And although they understood the necessity, it was very hurtful that Alan should be questioned in ways that showed he was being treated as a murder suspect. Most hurtful of all was the requirement that Ann look at two of the lewd photographs and listen to a few minutes of the tape recording to identify Lesley Ann's appearance and voice. The police explain that it was absolutely essential that the unmistakable evidence of a mother's identification should be available. A cunning defence counsel might have argued that an aunt or uncle didn't know the little girl well enough to be absolutely sure. But the trauma stayed with Ann West for the remainder of her life.

There was sufficient evidence now to justify arresting Hindley and charging her with complicity in the murders. The Transport Police leaked the information that some highly compromising material relating to murders and missing children had been sent down to Hyde. The western side of today's Greater Manchester borders a multiplicity of old constabulary districts and county boundaries. Hyde is in Cheshire. Ashton-under-Lyne is in Lancashire. The Manchester City Police were not directly responsible for Manchester Central Station, but the Transport Police's lines and platforms ran through their bailiwick. Saddleworth Moor extended into what is now West Yorkshire. Had Hindley and Brady only driven south as well as north-east from home, they would have brought in Derbyshire. An impressive array of CID top brass from competing forces was rapidly assembled in Hyde's tiny police station. Chief Superintendent Benfield, who had possession of the suitcases and the arrested suspect, no longer considered sending the file on Brady to the courts and closing the case. The Cheshire Police were going to continue their investigations, and would be glad to cooperate with any other interested force.

Most interested was Detective Chief Inspector Joe Mounsey, head of Ashton-under-Lyne CID and the third man to play a major role in bringing the Moors Murderers to book. John Kilbride was a missing person on his caseload, and he had no doubt that Brady and Hindley had killed him and buried him on the moors. "A policeman's policeman" in the view of one of his subordinates, he had personal determination and the charisma to carry his men with him. He headed a team that went hunting over Saddleworth Moor, concentrating at first on the region where Patricia Hodges reported that Brady and Hindley had parked their van on the A635. The search method was primitive compared with more recent advances. Lines of police officers walked across the moorland, armed with rods and canes which they pushed into the ground and smelled to see whether any odour of decomposition came up.

The Press might well have felt that the police were playing "on again, off again" with them. Immense coverage had been requested when the children went missing, and in giving it the newspapers could feel that they had been helping the police by arousing public interest. Now that there was the possibility of a continuation to the story, they wanted to be there. But the police did not want pressmen distracting them and corrupting a crime scene, if they found one. So they took stringent measures to try to keep cameramen at a distance.

Within a day of Patricia Hodges pointing them in the right direction, they struck lucky. On October 16 dusk was setting in by mid-afternoon, and the searching teams were preparing to return to their coaches and pack up. PC Bob Spears made one last trek up to a hilltop. He wanted a pee, but he also feels that something was drawing him to that spot. His colleagues were shouting to him to hurry up so that they could get home, but what looked like a stick projecting from a water-filled depression caught his eye. He prodded around it and realized there was a body of some sort there. It might well be a sheep. But he refused to return until others had come to help him examine it.

They dug channels through the peat to drain the water out of the depression. They started turning the soil. And they found Lesley Ann Downey. The "stick" was her weathered forearm.

Now Mounsey had proved the first point: there were bodies on the moors. He was determined to find John Kilbride's, and spent a lot of his own time going up to the moors and trying to decide where it might be hidden. He studied the photographs in the suitcases and decided that one, which showed Myra Hindley crouching in front of an outcrop of stones with her little dog Puppet nestled in her coat, was significant. For it seemed that she was not looking at Puppet, but at a spot in front of her where the soil might have been disturbed. This might be a grave site. But where exactly was the picture taken? Even if the outcrop could be identified, the focal depth of the camera lens could distort distances and make it impossible to judge how far in front of them Hindley had been positioned.

To solve the problem Mounsey turned to the fourth contributor to a major "result" in this case: Scenes of Crime Officer (SoCO) Mike Massheder. He was a photographer. The task of reproducing John Kilbride's picture for mass circulation had fallen to him in 1963. And he had undertaken the rather dull job of printing more and more pictures of empty moorland landscapes from Brady's negatives. But on being asked to enhance the picture of Hindley and Puppet, he realized that the sky in the background was over-exposed. To find out whether the blank whiteness of the print (or blackness of the negative) might conceal useful detail, Massheder masked the foreground section with his hand while he blasted a strong jolt of light through the enlarger and negative on to print paper before dropping it in developer. And the old trick worked. A faint outline of distant hills was revealed in the background. These could be triangulated with the stone outcrop, which had been iden-tified as Hollin Brow Knoll when Massheder's colleague Ray Gelder went to take pictures on the moor and realized that a stone forma-tion in front of him was the one he had seen in the picture of Hindley. Massheder set up his cameras as near as possible to the spot where Brady seemed to have taken his snapshot. And by pro-ducing an almost identical picture he confirmed that the police had found the right spot to dig. John Kilbride's body was recovered, just 400 yards from Lesley Ann Downey's, on the other side of the road.

Massheder also did some work on the Lesley Ann pictures. With just a blank wall, a white sheet and a bit of a bedhead as back-ground, there was nothing to prove where the little girl had been taken to and photographed. But Massheder carefully enlarged and enhanced the image of the bedhead, and by careful comparison with marks and knocks on Hindley's bed was able to prove that it was the one where the child had been tormented.

Massheder was a police officer doing an aide-to-CID job that has since been civilianized as one of Sir Harold Scott's reforms, which started in London in the1950s. The argument ran that investigators who simply collected fingerprints, expertly photographed scenes of crime and vacuumed up or scraped together dust and other parti-cles for microscopic analysis didn't need the power of arrest, knowl-edge of criminal law, sworn commitment to uphold the Queen's Peace and experience of pounding the pavements which went to make a police detective. The policy had enfuriated "Mr Fingerprints", Fred Cherrill, who resigned early from the police rather than head a bureau including civilian investigators. SoCOs from Massheder's day sometimes feel that being operational police officers gave them that little bit of extra motivation that counted. But present-day SoCO Ron Stocks points out that "expertise in scenes of crime has grown" so that whereas in the 1960s you were lucky if a detective had time to come and test an ordinary crime scene for fingerprints, today "virtually every burglary is attended by a scenes of crime officer who examines for forensic and fingerprint clues". In a sensitive murder case, full body protective clothing is likely to be worn, compared with the rubber gloves of 1924–64.

Colleagues of Mike Massheder's did further work tying Brady and Hindley inexorably to the incriminating materials in the suitcases. A fingerprint of Hindley's was found on one of the photographs of Lesley Ann. The negative of the picture of Hindley and Puppet on the moors was examined microscopically to prove beyond question that minute scrape marks from the metal plate supporting the film had been made by Brady's camera, and no other. There was a case to go to trial.

The trial at Chester Crown Court was a sensation. The defendants' absolutely frozen demeanour and chilling refusal to admit any responsibility or show any concern about the distress they had caused made them seem the most evil murderers anyone could imagine, even though the charming Haigh and charmless Christie had been equally heartless. But these two were young. They were young lovers, of all things. Two older-generation writers, who did not usually deal with crime, wrote books whose titles expressed their horror at the Moors Murderers. Her book was *On Iniquity*, said Pamela Hansford Johnson. *Beyond Belief*, cried Emlyn Williams. And both showed fears that Hindley and Brady represented a new depravity. Williams was much exercised by allegations that as an adolescent, Brady had watched himself masturbating in mirrors. Hansford Johnson thought decadence was running riot in northern England when she saw a young couple making love in a doorway after dark. Like Charles Manson in America, Hindley became a symbol of evil partly because she seemed to belie the innocence behind the sixties liberation of "sex, drugs, and rock 'n' roll".

But it was the tape that chilled the blood of an entire country. The voice of a little girl screaming, crying, begging to be allowed to go home to her mother. The frozen voice of Hindley telling her to shut up, to do what she was told, threatening to hit her, telling her to "put it in". Ominous thumps and bangs in the background. Hindley subsequently came to care about other people's opinion of her, and said, "It's not what you think" or "It's not as bad as you think", and claimed that the background noises are just Ian setting up photographic equipment. But there can be no apologizing away this dreadful creation, which, as Ian Fairley observes, still has an overpowering effect when played in training exercises to tough classes of experienced detectives who think they've seen and heard everything there is to know about evil. Fairley adds that one of the most chilling things is the cosy topping and tailing of the piece with the merry Christmas hit "The Little Drummer Boy". This was this frightful couple's idea of a work of art. The only human moment either of them showed throughout the trial came when Hindley was asked by counsel what she felt when she heard the tape played to the court. And in a low voice she said, "I am ashamed."

For the most part they accepted their detachment from the rest of humanity, gloried in their perverted love for each other and their half-witted pseudo-Nietzschean philosophy of cruelty, domination and neo-Nazism that Brady had cobbled together. And they denied all responsibility. Brady said Smith was responsible for almost everything and Hindley was entirely innocent. Hindley said she didn't know anything about it, except that Brady wasn't responsible. They were convicted and went to life sentences with the judge privately observing that if the Home Office paid any attention to his opinion they would never walk free again.

Not long after their committal to prison, Hindley was overheard in Holloway falsely accusing David Smith of helping them murder a 16-year-old girl – which she and Brady had done. This had to be Pauline Reade, whose disappearance from her home two doors away from the Smiths in July 1963 had constituted the first of Manchester's "missing children" stories. Inevitably, then, there was speculation that Hindley and Brady might have been responsible for the disappearance of 12-year-old Keith Bennett on June 16, 1964.

DCI Mounsey was a first-rate copper in public relations, as well as in dogged detective determination. He made a point of keeping in touch with the Kilbride family, visiting when there was no apparent need, just to reassure them that authority still cared. This was very important as the victims' families, encouraged by the tabloid press, held themselves together as a cohesive group agitating for renewed searches on the moors to find Pauline's and Keith's bodies, and insisting that there should be no remission of sentence for the murderers: life must mean life. Irresponsible journalists encouraged them to indulge in hysterical outbursts, but although this once led Danny Kilbride to say Hindley "was dead" if she came out and got near him, he concedes that he is not a man of violence, and is generally satisfied that the continued agitation will ensure that she is not released.

The Wests, by contrast, prompted by nothing but their own erroneous gut feeling that David Smith was concealing knowledge of other murders, went round to the Smiths' home and started a fight. Afterwards a policewoman visited the Wests with a plastic bag full of hanks of Maureen Smith's hair that Ann West had torn out, and asked cynically what she thought she was doing – making a wig? Both Ann and Alan West thought this rather funny, and were not especially grateful for the consideration which, in the light of what they had gone through, let them off with a caution.

Up to 1970 Hindley and Brady were sustained by *folie à deux*: a hysterical condition in which their mutual love led them to increasingly confident belief that their antisocial actions and beliefs were right, and everybody else was wrong. But in 1970 Hindley fell out of love with Brady. From then on her energies were bent toward winning her freedom, and Brady's focused on stopping her. The benevolent former cabinet minister Lord Longford, who had always made prison-visiting part of his Christian duties, was one of the few people who saw both Hindley and Brady regularly, and when Hindley converted to Roman Catholicism he started to urge that her sentence be remitted. His call was premature and provoked counter-demands that she should never be released. Hindley wasn't helped when a prison governor ill-advisedly took her for a walk in the park in 1972, preparatory to anticipated release. This virtually compelled the Home Secretary to say that no such release was likely to be forthcoming. The following year Hindley was found plotting escape with the connivance of a prison officer who had become her lesbian lover. Brady, by contrast, let it be known that he neither expected nor wanted to be released ever.

When Maureen Smith died prematurely of a stroke in 1977, the Wests went to the funeral convinced that Hindley would be let out of jail to attend it. And, equally wrongly convinced that they had seen her among the mourners, they started an unseemly brawl.

Serious journalists started to ask questions about other murders. Had Hindley and Brady killed Pauline Reade and Keith Bennett? Had Brady killed a fellow inmate of borstal who disappeared? Had he and Smith conspired to carry out a murder as well as the admitted bank robbery they planned? Hindley denied everything, and petitioned for her release. Brady wouldn't comment.

In 1983 journalist Frederick Harrison wrote a piece on Brady's weight loss in prison which impressed Lord Longford. Most journalists treated Hindley and Brady as moral subhumans and, from Longford's standpoint as a Christian who acknowledged all people to be sinful, were unbearably Pharisaical. Many were downright deceptive or hypocritical. But Harrison impressed Longford as genuine, and Longford introduced him to Brady. In a sequence of eight personal interviews Harrison learned that Brady was disgusted by Hindley's manipulative claims of innocence and wanted to expose her as involved in the murders of Keith Bennett and Pauline Reade. Hindley had picked up Pauline on the way to a dance, asking her to come and help her look for a lost glove on the moors. Keith had been abducted on the way to his grandmother's just a few minutes' walk from where he lived. Brady did not, however, give details of how they were killed, or of his own bisexual paedophile assaults on all the children and young people. (Forensic science established that even Edward Evans had been naked with Brady before David Smith arrived to find them both fully clothed again.) He did admit to his own murder of "a wino" – a confession that the police have never been able to support with the finding of an unidentified body or a report of a missing person. At the same time Harrison noted that Brady was so severely ill that his communication at times was reduced to an incomprehensible whining noise. He decided to campaign for proper psychiatric treatment for Brady, and still feels that this distinguishes his articles from the merely sensational pieces which tricked the murderers into making marketable statements. Harrison would have liked to wait longer and learn more before publishing. But the editor of the *People* learned that he was sitting on the scoop of repeated taped interviews with Brady, and insisted that they be brought out immediately.

When Harrison's articles appeared in the summer of 1985, the Home Office wanted to know what the Greater Manchester Police were going to do about the confessions relating to Keith Bennett and Pauline Reade. Detective Chief Superintendent Peter Topping, head of the Manchester CID, along with the deputy head of Cheshire CID, went to interview Brady. But he proved totally uncooperative. It was not until November the following year that Topping decided to interview Hindley. Every mention of her still stirred up a hornets' nest of indignation and criticism, and created more distress for the victims' families.

This was the very worst moment in the history of the Greater

Manchester Police. Their controversial Chief Constable, James Anderton, was in the throes of a spiritual crisis which would lead him to leave the Methodist Church and convert to Catholicism, and he was starting to make extremely ill-advised public pronouncements about AIDS being God's retribution for the "cesspit" of moral degenerates and homosexuals, and about his personal belief that God spoke through him. His deputy, John Stalker, had just been returned to duty from suspension on trumped-up allegations of associating with criminals and misusing official cars. Journalists' investigation of the case convinced the public that Stalker was the victim of an establishment conspiracy to prevent him from completing his investigation of malpractices by the Royal Ulster Constabulary and the security forces in Northern Ireland. The suspension had ruined cordial relations between Anderton and Stalker. Topping had been promoted to effective operational command of the CID in Stalker's absence and against his wishes. When Anderton let Topping pursue Harrison's revelations without informing Stalker, who had been part of the original Moors Murders team, it was easy for sections of the press to assume that this was a desperate attempt to distract attention from disarray at the top of the force, and possibly win some goodwill, which Anderton patently lacked, at a time when Stalker was enjoying enormous public esteem for his integrity and dignity.

The peculiar timing of the renewed search on Saddleworth lent colour to the theory that "Stalker's enemies" wanted to drag the spotlight away from him. The beginning of winter was a daft time to start searching moorland that would soon be freezing and impossible to dig up. But former Detective Inspector Geoffrey Knupfer, Topping's assistant on the case, explains that the timing was intended to put pressure on Hindley. The police had been advised that she was going to be very uncooperative. So Topping and Knupfer decided to go and interview her, and immediately hold a press conference outside Cookham Wood Prison to say that "in the light of the interview" they were going to start searching Saddleworth Moor again. They knew perfectly well that the weather would allow them just two weeks on the moor, but calculated that if Hindley had to sit through the winter with the knowledge that the police were going to start digging again in the spring, she would be unnerved and probably look for a little goodwill by helping them.

The "cunning plan" (as Geoff Knupfer has called it, consciously echoing Baldrick from *Blackadder*) collapsed underneath them like an unlocked door crashing open to a shoulder charge. They had been misinformed about Hindley. She was very willing to cooperate. And Topping and Knupfer still had to tell the press what they had promised and then start a search which had little hope of finding anything before it shut down for three months.

The Press came out in force hoping for pictures of Hindley on the moors. When she was flown up in a Metropolitan Police helicopter in December, the situation was hopeless. The weather turned misty, with a little snow, and Hindley was quite unable to orientate herself. Press helicopters hovered overhead until the Met helicopter was ordered to take up a position 100 feet above the search party to keep the flying photographers at bay. Subsequently some of the newspapers threatened to sue the police for dangerous flying. And when the search was resumed in the spring and dragged on into the summer, the press turned furious fire on the police.

Brady's obstructive position cracked slightly when he saw the publicity Hindley was receiving. Now he offered to help the police, but on his own terms. He wanted a weekend out of prison in a flat with alcohol and television. Failing that, he wanted the means with which to kill himself. It was obvious that he was more interested in manipulating the situation to keep as much control as possible than in helping anybody else. There was never the faintest possibility of his terms being met.

Several factors contributed to the successful search. Hindley, whose original cooperation had been limited to talking about "areas of interest to Ian," finally came clean and made complete confessions to the five murders, giving details of where and how the children were abducted, and where and how Brady had killed and buried them. She insisted that she had never been present at any of the murders: she had always been back at the car keeping a lookout, or in another room. The victims' families have never believed these protestations of limited culpability. The police, who have always found that everything that can be checked in Hindley's statements has proved true, keep an open mind. In the one murder that was witnessed by another person, David Smith actually confirms her claim to have been "in another room" at the fatal moment, though he also makes it quite clear why she must – as she does – accept responsibility as an active and necessary confederate.

The police were able to get Hindley back on the moors again in the spring. Now she was honestly looking for the grave sites of Pauline Reade and Keith Bennett. But in a bleak landscape that seems to alter its shape seasonally as wind and rain hammer at the peaty soil, she was not able to do more than indicate vague areas at first. Pauline's body was somewhere in Hollin Brow Knoll, where John and Lesley Ann had been buried. Keith's was in a gully near the confluence of Shiney Brook and Hoe Grain. The searchers were immediately faced with the problem that had confronted Mounsey when he looked at the photo of Hindley on Hollin Brow Knoll. Just where, on the large outcrop of peat, was the grave site? They tried to eliminate areas that could be seen from the road, and then it occurred to somebody that the light could make a considerable difference. So they telephoned Hindley in prison and asked whether Pauline had been buried by daylight, and she recalled quite clearly that it was dusk, because she could just make out the silhouette of hills across the valley against the sky. That casual aside gave the clue that was needed. There were only a couple of places on the knoll from which the hills could be seen.

The police had the assurance of Professor Mike Green that the bodies were likely to have been preserved well if they were in peat. The light acidity of peat acted like a tannery on the skin, turning it to leather, while the fatty flesh turned to adipocere, a soapy substance which lasts for a long time in water. There was more sophisticated searching equipment than there had been 20 years before, and there would be no poking sticks into the peat and smelling the ends. But the bodies were past the stage of rapid decomposition, so thermal equipment to detect the heat produced by the process wouldn't work. Ground-penetrating radar showed up too many anomalies in the soil. Sniffer dogs trained to hunt out bodies were much more selective, even though there was always the likelihood that they would be drawn to dead sheep or rabbits. Yet even they proved impossible to use. The strong scent of peat masked the flesh odours from them. The police turned to archaeologists for advice.

Pegging and taping out a grid to chart the position of finds had been practised in the Christie case. British field archaeologists then gave the police a crash course in searching the ground scrupulously on their hands and knees with trowels. It was even more labour-intensive than a fingertip search of the surface. Somebody heard of an American archaeologist at the Smithsonian Institute called Bruno Frolich who had worked successfully with police searchers, and he arrived from a dig in the Middle East like a breath of fresh air.

"Oh, throw the pointing trowels away and get the spades out!" he said. "Otherwise you're gonna be for ever, and what you're looking for is evidence of a crime, not a museum exhibit." This advice was invaluable. On July 1 a spade touched something in the peat. Clearance with a trowel showed a foot in a white stiletto shoe:

something Pauline Reade was known to have been wearing when she disappeared. Careful excavation brought up her body, preserved as wrinkled leather and adipocere, just as Mike Green had predicted. Professor Green now turned to leather-workers and archaeologists for advice on restoring the body to something more like its original condition. They recommended a bath in polyethylene glycol. And although this could not restore colour, it did soften and elasticize the skin, so that it was possible to determine that Pauline had probably been strangled after being sexually abused, just as Hindley's statement had claimed.

The discovery of Pauline's body had an immediate effect on Brady. He was working to his own agenda as usual, and far more interested in putting down Hindley than alleviating the suffering of Keith Bennett's relatives. But now he offered to come out on the moors without preconditions and identify Keith's resting place. When he strode off purposefully toward Shiney Brook, the police were confident that they would soon be uncovering the last body. When he stopped and said something to the effect of "Can you move that hill out of the way?" they realized that Brady's mental disorder was far worse than they had imagined and that he was incapable of giving them any proper directions.

And Keith's body never has been found. The police completely dug up every single gully at the confluence of Shiney Brook and Hoe Grain, inundating the area but finding nothing. The soil there is not peaty, so the tannic acid that contributed to preserving the other bodies is lacking. Boys' bodies, with less fat distributed over them than girls', are less prone to convert to adipocere. The belief of the police and their advisers is that they must have turned over Keith's grave, but his body had decomposed beyond recognition. Winnie Johnson, his mother, and Danny Kilbride, John's brother, are not satisfied that this can be true. A belt buckle, a plastic button – something, they argue – must have survived. But Peter Topping was taken off the case and could not command the resources to continue searching. Nobody is likely to put up the funding for renewed excavation. And Winnie Johnson is forced to leave flowers at random points on the moors, to symbolize her love for her lost and murdered son.

1966–1980

THE AGE OF INNOCENCE dribbled away down the drain after the Moors Murders. But it had not yet gone completely. We had not become so sophisticated in categorizing monstrous crime as to identify Hindley and Brady as serial killers or paedophiles: labels which would instantly be stuck on them today.

Yet even before they had been convicted, the fascination with killers who caused a long sequence of mysterious deaths was becoming evident. The Boston Strangler was succeeded by "Zodiac" in California, who attacked courting couples and wrote letters to the police signed with the supposedly astrological emblem of a cross covering a circle, but has never been identified. "Jack the Stripper" in London was succeeded by the equally unidentified "Bible John" in Glasgow. Like "Zodiac", the Glasgow murderer was seen and described. He shared a taxi with Helen Puttock and her sister Jeannie, and went on to murder Helen after Jeannie had left them. From Jeannie we know that he said his name was John and that his conversation was larded with references to the Bible –

especially Jesus's conversations with women supposedly practising adultery or bigamy. He killed three young women, all of whom he met at Barrowlands Ballroom; all of whose partially or fully unclothed bodies were found with sanitary towels they had been using discarded beside them. It seems that, like Norman John Collins, the student from Ypsilanti, Michigan, who was actively murdering girls around the same time (1967–69), the Glaswegian was in some way provoked by menstruation. Both these men, too, were young, healthy-looking and capable of striking up easy casual friendships with young women. The old stereotype of a sneaky, undersexed Christie look-alike as serial killer was finished. The panic engendered by Bible John's activities is said to have driven a number of young Scotsmen to emigrate to Canada when they came under the misplaced suspicion of their neighbours.

By the 1970s heterosexuals ceased to have the serial-killing field to themselves. Juan Corona murdered and mutilated 25 male migrant workers in California. Dean Corll murdered 27 boys in Texas. John Wayne Gacey ran out of room in the crawl-space beneath his Chicago home for the 33 or more boys he killed.

England's outstanding multiple murderer of the 1970s was the huge and uncontrollable Patrick Mackay. Like Peter Manuel, he was by habit a petty criminal and his murders did not fall into the sort of neat and observable pattern which creates panic. He certainly started killing in 1973, and by 1974 the police believe he had probably killed a girl student, certainly killed an old lady, and probably a middle-aged lady and a child. He never confessed to any of these murders, but he did admit to two subsequent killings in the course of his predation on elderly ladies in Chelsea. Mackay was a good-looking young half-Guyanese, who had excellent manners when he chose to use them. He stood 6 feet 4 inches tall by the time he was 20 in 1972. He would offer to carry old ladies' shopping, and when they let him into their flats, he stole what he could. When one was frightened by his manner and chained her door, refusing to admit him, he hurled himself at the door, snapped the chain and killed her. Such violent and lethal rage was his typical response to opposition. By the time he was 13 he had reached 6 feet, and had attempted to strangle his mother and his sister, as well as a smaller boy who annoyed him in the street. He was sent to a mental home which was legally obliged to discharge him when he reached 16, although the psychiatrists disapproved, recognizing him as "a cold-blooded psychopathic killer". Psychopaths might be described as people lacking any automatic internalized recognition of the difference between good and evil: they are aware of it objectively as something others define, but which they feel no compulsion to respect. Moreover, they have no intuitive perception of other people as anything but objects to be used or manipulated as best suits themselves. Their conduct often appears simply evil, without any need for psychological explanation. Yet they may, for their own easily perceived advantage, consistently accept the public pressure to conform and never in fact behave in any obviously unacceptable way. Psychopathy is defined as a "personality disorder" and not a disease, and psychopaths can neither be treated nor certified and incarcerated for their own and others' good. This apparent anomaly may perhaps be explained by comparing a personality disorder with a physical deformity. The latter may be an incurable handicap which does not compel the sufferer to lead an abnormal physical life. Byron became an outstanding boxer and swimmer despite the deformity of a club foot.

Mackay was caught in 1975 when he murdered Father Anthony Crean, a Catholic priest who had befriended him. Some coarse young friends of Mackay's attributed this to Crean's supposed homosexuality, and Mackay, enraged by the thought, rushed down to the priest's house in Gravesend and lay in wait for him. When Father Crean came home and saw Mackay looking threatening he tried to run away. The furious giant chopped him down with an axe, and pushed him under the bloody water of his bath. Since Mackay's association with Father Crean was well known, and he had served a short prison sentence for forging one of the priest's cheques, he was quickly arrested. He confessed to some but not all of his murders, denying the obvious killing of a shopkeeper in Finsbury Park, north London. He offered the extraordinary story that he had first robbed the old man and then gone back to the shop to find that somebody else had battered him with a lead pipe, and that was why his footprints were in his blood and the incriminating shoes he had thrown away were stained with it.

On the other hand, Mackay confessed to the spontaneous murder of a tramp he had met on Hungerford Bridge and thrown into the Thames. The lack of any suitable missing-person report or any body recovered from the river makes it seem that Mackay was simply making up a murder here.

His was a weirdly childish personality. In his early teens, when in the mental home, he insisted on taking a doll to bed with him. At the age of 20, fascinated by fascism, he was too unstable to be acceptable even to the rejects and losers of the British National Party or the Union of Fascists. So he compensated by making himself a cardboard and tinfoil helmet and breastplate, and parading in front of his bedroom mirror, calling himself "Skyresh Bolvolt I, Dictator of the World". There never seems to have been any overt sexual component in his crimes. He killed in the course of stealing pathetically small amounts. And his inability to tolerate any form of opposition seems better described as infantile rage – extremely dangerous in a young man of his size and strength – than as the will to control, which is nowadays seen as the serial killer's driving passion.

On reflection, though, it should be clear that some infantile fury must underlie even an overtly sexual killer's apparently placid surface when a man makes fearful assaults on 21 women, and kills 13 of them. That is what Peter Sutcliffe, the Yorkshire Ripper, embarked upon, just as Patrick Mackay was arrested and put out of harm's way. It gave this outwardly quiet, good-looking Bradford lorry driver a notoriety for which his own secret narcissism lusted. "In this truck is a man whose latent genius, if unleashed, would rock the nation, whose dynamic energy would overpower those around him. Better let him sleep?" ran the self-glorifying card he posted in the cab of his lorry. In fact his practice of bashing lone women over the head before partially exposing their breasts and private parts and stabbing them with a sharpened screwdriver revealed a sexually inadequate creature whose meek public acquiescence in the lifestyle preferred by his better-educated, house-proud and socially superior wife reflected the respectable "mummy's boy" image of him held by his more gregarious and volatile father and siblings.

His case became infamous for the supposed police incompetence which led to his being interviewed seven times but never included in the list of the most serious suspects. The notorious wild goose chase after a man with a Geordie accent who sent mocking letters and a cassette tape to George Oldfield, the Senior Investigating Officer, actually rested on powerful forensic evidence and the imaginative use of an academic expert. Traces of light machine oil found on the injuries to the victim Josephine Whittaker matched traces found on one of the letters, apparently confirming that the writer really was the killer. And asking the brilliant dialectologist Professor Stanley Ellis to pinpoint the home town indicated by the tape maker's accent was an impressively original piece of detective work. Of course, countless man-hours were lost down this dead end. And the immense publicity given to the voice on the tape, thanks to the co-operation of all the news media, ensured that the whole nation was aware that an enormous police effort had been dedicated to a false clue which just happened to insult Mr Oldfield. Yet even the most critical police officers, who felt from the start that this was misdirected effort, conceded that the West Yorkshire Police had no option but to follow up any leads supplied by the tape and letters. And unlike the general public, the police were aware that it spoke very well for "the system" that Sutcliffe showed up on it repeatedly. The only mistake lay in prioritizing the accent detected by Professor Ellis, so that the one report from an interviewing officer recommending Sutcliffe's transfer to the strongest suspect files was shelved.

Another brilliant and painstaking piece of detective work which was in process at the time when Sutcliffe was caught would surely have led to his arrest in short order. A new £5 note found in a secret compartment of Manchester victim Jean Jordan's handbag had been identified by the Mint and the transferring and issuing banks as one which had gone into a pay packet in West Yorkshire. But with 300 possible recipients (including Sutcliffe) identified and inter-viewed, it had not been possible to pinpoint suspicion. By 1980 Manchester Police had refined the trace by finding out exactly how each individual teller on the note's trail from the Mint to Yorkshire counted and stacked paper currency. This rerun reduced the num-ber of possible recipients to 30, and Sutcliffe would have been due for a renewed interrogation with changed guidelines giving a low priority to the supposed Geordie accent.

As the police themselves proudly observed, however, the Yorkshire Ripper was ultimately arrested as a result of "good old-fashioned coppering". This was the simplest and most basic form of observation: the beat patrol's (or, in this case, patrol car's) normal open eye for anything untoward, which spotted a parked car holding a known prostitute and her punter, apparently preparing to perpetrate an act of public indecency. Technical routine checking with the DVLA computer showed that the car was using stolen number plates, and Sutcliffe was swiftly taken into custody. Here his demeanour instantly aroused suspicion and brought him before the Ripper enquiry team for interrogation, which led to his confession and conviction.

The lessons of the Yorkshire Ripper affair were not lost on the police. The first and most important was the way the investigation had become swamped by the weight of information: the impossibility of accessing and cross-referencing relevant statements and reports which had led to the scandal of Sutcliffe's never appearing in the file of serious suspects. The obvious answer was computers to communicate with each other. The Home Office approved, four years after Sutcliffe's arrest.

"The HOLMES system – the spur to produce that as a computer programme arose out of the misfortunes of the Ripper," says Chief Superintendent Dick Holland, who served on the Yorkshire Ripper case from start to finish. "And it's said that if there hadn't been a Ripper … then the Home Office would have had to invent one to get the system to work with electronic filing and indexing and electronic retrieval on a computer." HOLMES is the "Home Office Large Major Enquiries System", and, yes, the acronym was intended to suggest Sherlock. It is crucial today, as Dick Holland observes, "because of the movement, the diverse mobility of the modern population [and] the modern criminal". By the end of the century it was supplemented by "the police computer" – actually a mass of different computerized data held by different forces on different systems, and including Criminal Records, Local Intelligence and even things like Standing Orders and gazetted information that used to be printed for circulation. And, of course, rapid access to DVLA basic records, such as had nailed Sutcliffe's stolen number plates.

Equally useful to Large Major Enquiries was the Scimitar programme introduced at Bramshill Police College. This gives senior officers special training in the efficient management of massive investigations. Never again did the police want to see a dedicated and committed Assistant Chief Constable work himself to the point of a heart attack, only to have the press and public jeer at him for having lost 18 months by single-minded concentration on a wrong lead. Computerization and managerial training were both recommended by Her Majesty's Inspector of Constabulary following an official review of the case. He also urged the standardization of procedures, as well as the use of advisory teams and of specialist and scientific support. It seems a little hard that an investigation which learned from a PhD student all about the habits of tricolera flies, in an attempt to see whether specific rare maggots on one victim's body pointed to a countryman killer, should be accused of undervaluing specialist support. And it is deeply ironic that they should be urged to lean more firmly on that forensic science which had misled them with the light engineering oil found in Josephine Whittaker's wounds and on the malicious hoaxer's envelope.

During the investigation a senior officer on the case had met the FBI psychological profilers Robert Ressler and John Douglas at Bramshill, where they were giving visiting lectures. Despite the Englishman's suspicion of this American "voodoo", they gave him an informal assessment based on the limited information he could put before them, and suggested (accurately, as it turned out), that the perpetrator was not the author of the letters and tape, but would be found to live in the West Yorkshire area and to be employed as some sort of driver – Post Office, trucking, even perhaps police. Contrary to some reports, however, this analysis was never passed on to the enquiry and was overruled. It was simply a friendly conversation in a pub. The new technique was not formally adopted in England until Professor Paul Britton drifted into a version of it, almost accidentally around 1986.

The other great development of the 1980s would be DNA "genetic fingerprinting", actually discovered and developed in England. This offered a more sophisticated and exact way of proving that body cells came from an individual than the highly complex advanced blood grouping worked out and refined by Margaret Pereira and Brian Culliford in the Metropolitan Police Forensic Science Laboratory in the 1960s.

But when the next serial killer after the Yorkshire Ripper was exposed, the police still had no local computer system available for a murder task force. The personal computer was not a standard household item in 1983, and the layman still thought of its most important use as replacing the electric typewriter. When the Senior Investigating Officer asked for "a word processor" to manage data in the Dennis Nilsen case, his request was considered and rejected on the grounds that its cost could not be justified. Ironically, this was a Metropolitan Police view, although Scotland Yard had been called in on an earlier case that swamped police card-indexing facilities. This was the Cannock Chase murders of 1967, when three separate constabularies failed to liaise properly and it was by luck as much as judgement that Raymond Morris was caught before his murder of two little girls could positively increase to three, bringing him into the category of "serial killer".

Fortunately the great serial-killing case exposed in 1983 could be managed on the card-indexed carousels. It was the last Large Major Enquiry in London to do so. But then Dennis Nilsen's was the case that ran backwards: the case where the police had a murderer bang to rights, and then had the really difficult job of finding his victims.

DENNIS NILSEN

IF THERE WERE A PRIZE for the shortest police interrogation leading to a murderer's confession, Detective Chief Inspector Peter Jay would be a leading contender. And he himself would congratulate pathologist Professor David Bowen for an instant diagnosis from minimal evidence, and Detective Inspector Steve McCusker for a penetrating follow-up question.

On February 9, 1983 DCI Jay was called from his office to go to 23 Cranley Gardens, Muswell Hill, north London, where a Dyno-Rod drain cleaner had made an unpleasant discovery. At the end of the previous working day Mike Cattran had been sent to the house, where toilets were backing up when flushed. The three-storey building had been converted into flats. The two on the ground floor and one on the top floor were occupied; the middle of the house was empty. When Cattran's instruments showed that the blockage started in the soil pipe halfway up the house, he knew that something flushed from the top flat had created the problem. When he went down a manhole to an inspection pit, he found it full of lumps of meat that seemed dreadfully human. He was quite thankful that a telephone call to his office brought him instructions to go away and sleep on it and see whether it still looked sinister in the cold light of morning.

But on Wednesday February 9 the inspection pit had been cleared. In a drain Cattran found just three pieces of flesh and two or three bones that looked like knucklebones. Occupants of the ground-floor flats told him that they had heard the upstairs tenant moving around all night. It would transpire that he had been repeatedly flushing the toilets, then going to the inspection pit and clearing it. Now he had gone to work. They didn't know where. They didn't know what his job was.

DCI Jay put the remains in a plastic bag and drove them over to Professor Bowen at the new Charing Cross Hospital in Hammersmith. Perhaps these were human, he suggested. After 10 minutes' examination, Professor Bowen said, "You're absolutely right. They are human, and I can tell you that your victim has been strangled."

"I think you've been watching too much television!" said Jay.

And Bowen smiled, and said, "No. By pure chance you've brought me a bit of a neck, and there's a clear ligature mark on it."

Jay promptly got a search warrant and returned to Cranley Gardens with Detective Inspector Steve McCusker and Detective Constable Geoff Butler. They didn't go into the flat, however. A noisy dog barking there persuaded them to wait for the return of the occupant, 37-year-old Dennis Nilsen, an officer of the Manpower Services Commission stationed at the Kentish Town Job Centre. He arrived at about half past five, "looking just like Mr Ordinary", says the former Chief Inspector. "He was in a grey suit, he had spectacles and a scarf thrown round his neck, and as he came in I said to him light-heartedly, 'I'm Detective Chief Inspector Jay from Hornsey Police Station. I've come about your drains.'"

Given the odd and sinister nature of the discovery, Jay had decided that an initial light tone would be the best way of avoiding a panic or violent reaction.

Dennis Nilsen smiled. "Since when have the police been interested in blocked drains?" he asked.

"You take me up in your flat and I'll tell you," replied Jay. As they went up the stairs, Nilsen asked whether McCusker and Butler were health inspectors. He didn't react to learning they were police officers. In the flat, Jay carried out his miniature interrogation:

Q. Mr Nilsen, your drains were blocked with human remains.

A. Oh, my God! How awful!

Q. [Moving closer] Now don't mess me about. Where's the rest of the body?

A. They're in two plastic bags in the other room. I'll show you.

Q. I thought so. What's been going on here?

A. It's a long story. I'll tell you everything.

Q. No, don't show me now. I'm going to arrest you on suspicion of murder.

As the car took the party back to the police station, McCusker reflected on Nilsen's curious response to the question about "the rest of the body".

"They're in two plastic bags," he had said.

"Are we talking about one body or two?" McCusker asked suddenly.

Nilsen took his gaze off the passing traffic and said calmly, "Neither. It's 16." Jay's hands flew off the steering wheel, and he had to recover himself quickly and turn his mind to keeping the car in its lane.

This instant success brought certain problems with it. Ever since habeas corpus, England has been unwilling to allow citizens to languish in custody without demonstrated reason. The police had 48 hours to find sufficient corroborative evidence to put before a magistrate and persuade the court to commit Nilsen for trial, or remand him in custody while further investigation continued. Sir Robert Anderson, who headed the Jack the Ripper enquiry, had been vocal in his regret that the British police did not have the Continental right to hold a suspect indefinitely during the search for evidence.

Of those 48 hours, 24 had to be sacrificed before the Scenes of Crime team could examine the location for fingerprints. Nilsen had left his windows open to minimize smells and so his flat was covered with damp, which made the use of fingerprint powder impossible. Ron Stocks was the Scenes of Crime Officer handling the case, and he had to bring in industrial heaters for a full day before he could get to work. Even then he felt that the place smelt surprisingly fresh, and was impressed by Nilsen's inclusion of bathroom airfreshener blocks in all his grisly packages. By contrast, Jay had been struck by the whiff of decaying flesh as soon as he went in. The two contrasted equally in their estimates of the rather uncomfortable bachelor pad: Jay thought it was squalidly untidy; Stocks thought this was true of the kitchen, although he saw the rest as sparsely furnished and anything but cosy, but rather obsessively ordered.

Fortunately Nilsen was cooperative and told them where the remains were hidden. Two big plastic bin liners in the wardrobe held body parts; suitcases in tea chests held bones and three boiled heads. A bathroom unit that looked permanent concealed a pair of legs. With just one hour to spare, sufficient evidence went to a magistrate to have Nilsen remanded in police custody for a further nine days, and the more detailed work could be undertaken, such as examining the bath and lavatory outflow pipes for blood and tissue.

Once Nilsen was charged, the police were unable to turn to the press for the sort of help that publicity can supply in a hunt for the truth. Saying anything more than "a man has been charged" could prejudice his trial. If there really were 16 bodies stashed away somewhere, consideration for relatives' sensitivities demanded that there be some restraint on the cameramen who would besiege the scene of crime. Jay's hope that the quick and quiet arrest after nightfall might escape press attention was dashed by Mike Cattran's friendship with Frances Hardy, a young reporter on a local paper in Bishop's Stortford. Muswell Hill was outside her readership area, but she prepared a brief and professional bulletin and sent it to five national tabloids. In Fleet Street, Douglas Bence of the *Daily Mirror* picked it up and turned it into a page-five story. This led the rest of the press to Cranley Gardens in a rush. From now on the police would have to start their searches before dawn to avoid photographers, but finish before the early encroaching winter dusk. In the meantime, some lucky householders in the two north London streets where, it turned out, Nilsen had disposed of bodies were able to cut good deals with television news crews, renting out rooms as location bases.

Unfortunately the *Sun* ran the screaming headline "POLICE BLUNDER" just as the jury were going to consider their verdict. This referred to the discovery of a heart, lungs and windpipe in a street litter bin, months before Nilsen was arrested. The finder, an anatomist, was sure they were human. The police he called believed them to be animal, and kept no record of the incident. There is no obvious reason to believe it would have led anyone to Nilsen in any case. The newspaper slur on their work was deeply resented by Jay and Detective Chief Superintendent Geoffrey Chambers, who had conducted a textbook, snag-free investigation from the moment they were called in.

One of the oddest features of their perfection was a prelude to the interviewing procedure. Naturally it was going to take some time to take statements about an alleged 16 murders. Before the first session, Nilsen was made to strip naked and had his body examined by a doctor who recorded every mark on it. These were then photographed. This was repeated before each interview the police held with him. It was not an attempt at humiliation or intimidation, but the necessary response to an ever-increasing habit of defendants to withdraw confessions made in police stations with the false claim that they had been beaten out of them. A few years later the Police and Criminal Evidence Act would result in most serious interviews being audio- or video-taped to obviate constant legal battles over the rectitude of police interrogation.

An immediate difficulty the investigation faced was that Nilsen genuinely didn't know who most of his victims were. He had picked them up from the transient population wandering through gay pubs and accepting beds for the night from any stranger who offered hospitality. He had killed 12 of them in his previous flat at 195 Melrose Avenue, Willesden. Living on the ground floor and with the use of a garden, he had been able to hold three big bonfires in the middle of the night, disposing of bodies he had stashed under his floorboards and adding car tyres to overpower the smell. This required a team of police cadets to make fingertip searches of the garden, during which they recovered over a thousand bone fragments, but nothing which could positively identify any of the victims. It also earned them some tetchy criticism from archaeologists who thought their recovery approach was unprofessional and risked losing evidence. Wisely, the police paid no attention.

In the course of a long series of short interviews, Nilsen was able to give five names. Stephen Sinclair was his last victim, a hopeless, drug-abusing drifter with a long record of convictions for petty thefts and, in his early years, half-hearted arson attempts. One of his fingers remained among the body parts found in Cranley Gardens, and his identity was quickly confirmed by the Fingerprint Bureau at Scotland Yard. The murder of Stephen Sinclair was the first offence with which Nilsen was formally charged.

Only one of his victims was not a drifter. A young Canadian

whom he knew as Ken had been in London on holiday in 1979, and met Nilsen at the Princess Louise pub in High Holborn, where there was live jazz. He intended to visit his uncle in Sussex the following day, and collect the money banked with him for his ticket home. After the music he agreed to go home with Nilsen to listen to some records. He was sitting in a chair in the Melrose Avenue flat with a stereo headset on when Nilsen strangled him with its flex. Chief Superintendent Chambers, as it happened, knew all about Ken Ockenden. He had been in charge of the CID at King's Cross in 1980. A reliable young man who maintained close contact with his family, Ken had been reported missing when he failed to turn up in Sussex. His parents had come over from Canada to help with the search. Nothing had suggested a deliberate disappearance. No accident report pointed to his end. Inspector Roy Davis said presciently, "There is a very strong possibility that this young man was murdered, and his body, so far, successfully concealed." Of fifteen thousand missing persons on police files between 1973 and 1980, Ken Ockenden was one of only two Nilsen victims to be reported missing. The killer trawled in a social stratum of near-anonymity where friends were transient and families did not expect to hear from them.

Malcolm Barlow could be traced through a Good Samaritan moment on Nilsen's part. Like Stephen Sinclair, the young drifter was epileptic, and Nilsen, out walking his dog Bleep, came across the young man sitting on the low wall outside Melrose Avenue recovering from a fit. Nilsen called an ambulance and Barlow was taken to Willesden General Hospital. In the evening he came back to thank Nilsen, who invited him in to have something to eat. Nilsen gave him an omelette, and there followed one of the rare occasions when Nilsen offered some sort of motive for a murder. Barlow insisted on drinking beer with his meal. Nilsen thought this was unacceptable, since the hospital had given him medication

which contraindicated alcohol. Barlow said he didn't care. Nilsen
told author Brian Masters that in that case he didn't care either. He
told the police that he didn't want the embarrassment of calling
another ambulance and having its crew find Barlow dying of the
mixture of alcohol and medication. And for this "reason" he
strangled him.

Martyn Duffey looked likely to be an easy target for police to
trace. A "Martin Duffy" would have been much harder. Nilsen was
sure of his name. The young man had trained as a chef and carried
a set of initialled knives which Nilsen used for some time, before
cunningly letting them rust and then junking them. The unusual
spellings led the police to feel sure they'd made an identification
when a Martyn Duffey turned up on the missing-person files in
Derby. But shown a photograph, Nilsen said this was not the man
he had killed. Not until the police traced Duffey's separated parents
in Birkenhead and obtained a picture from them could they confirm that they had identified another of Nilsen's victims.

"A Scotsman called Billy Sutherland" gave the police some very
solid work. The Edinburgh Central Registry Office reported that
there were 40 men of that name who would have been in their
twenties in the early 1980s. The police had eliminated 38 of them
before they traced the common-law wife of the right one. She and
Billy's son had not seen him for six years, and she had no idea that,
after she left him because she could not stand life in London, he
drifted on to the streets, becoming, in police terms, a "KAMP"
(Known As Male Prostitute) called "Doris" by his clients.

"John the Guardsman" was another of Nilsen's cryptic leads. This
man apparently came from High Wycombe. But not one of the five
Guards regiments had any record of a soldier called John from that
town. Again, it took a long effort of knocking on doors and asking
questions in High Wycombe and in gay pubs before the police
established that John Howlett, who had never been in the army in

his life, liked to dress in combat fatigues and pass himself off as a soldier.

The other Cranley Gardens victim (the second to be killed there) was identified by tried-and-tested forensic pathological and dental methods. Petty thief and drug addict Graham Allan was habitually getting into drunken fights, which he usually won. But in one of them he had broken his jaw. A hospital x-ray of the fracture survived, and could be matched with a plate of the skull among Nilsen's boiled heads. Allan's teeth could then be checked from dental records, and the identity of this man was established. Nilsen only remembered that he too was killed while eating an omelette: indeed, he couldn't remember why or even when and how he killed him. With his own characteristic black humour he remarked that he saw red weals on the corpse's neck, while unmasticated omelette protruded from its mouth. He knew the omelette couldn't have made the weals, he said, so he couldn't have "omeletted him to death".

Even before Howlett and Allan had been identified, the police were encouraged to let the case go to court and give up the expensive and almost impossible task of trying to identify further victims, described by Nilsen simply as "an Irishman" or "a skinhead" or a rentboy who looked half-Latino. Seven of Nilsen's victims can be named. Eight cannot. Nilsen has subsequently suggested that he confessed to three murders he hadn't committed because the police seemed to want him to. Psychologists who examined him can't say whether or not he may have committed more than the police estimate of 15 killings. Some writers wondered whether he had originally claimed 15 or 16 because he knew of Mary Ann Cotton, England's greatest multiple murderer at the time, who killed maybe 20 or more unwanted relatives in the nineteenth century, but was accorded 14 confirmed victims. Of the seven victims Nilsen named, only Kenneth Ockenden was missed by anybody.

The case against Nilsen was, however, very firmly established by "the ones that got away". Nilsen confessed to seven of these, some named, some unnamed. It proved possible to trace three and find evidence of two others. Three had actually reported violent incidents with Nilsen to the police. The first, Andrew Ho, was a cook who had left a restaurant in Soho after a row with the manager. He did not go to the police to complain about Nilsen. He went to confess that he feared he had seriously injured him. Going to Melrose Avenue in June 1979, between Nilsen's first murder in January of that year and his second in December, Ho had dozed off in a chair and woken to find his host tightening a tie around his neck. More by luck than judgement, he reached for a nearby brass candlestick and smashed it over Nilsen's head. Then he made his way out of the house, and the following day went to the police to confess his fear that he might have killed the man whose assault on him was still evident in the burn marks around his neck. The police went to Nilsen's house and found him alive and a little groggy. He said he'd had a number of people in the previous night, got very drunk, fell over and banged his head. Ho had no wish to proceed further. Nor did he wish to return from his new home in Switzerland to give evidence when Nilsen was finally arrested.

Another oriental chef who escaped was Toshimitsu Ozawa, a tourist on holiday in London. He had met a man called Desi in a pub, gone home with him, and fought off three assaults with a strangling tie. He showed the police the marks on his neck and demanded that this dangerous man be arrested. He dropped his complaint abruptly when he learned that he would have to stay in England to press charges and would put his job at risk by missing his flight home.

Stewart "Taffy" Coles did not get as far as the chair and the tie. He lived in Melrose Avenue, and was extremely surprised when Nilsen accosted him one night, knowing his name and a little about him.

The young Myra Hindley
with a friend

Myra Hindley with her dog Puppet

The sitting room in 16 Wardlebrook Avenue where Ian Brady
murdered Edward Evans

Ian Brady in
police custody

Hindley and Brady driven to prison in the same van after
the verdict

Maureen and David Smith, Myra's
sister and brother-in-law, whose
courage and determination brought
the murders to an end

Leeds University pathol-
ogist professor Cyril
Polson (2nd from right)
goes to help with the
original search for bodies
of Brady and Hindley's
victims on the moors

Brady (in dark glasses)
proved too mentally
disordered to give useful
assistance at this later search
for bodies on the moors

23 Cranley Gardens, the Muswell Hill house where Dennis Nilsen blocked the drains with his victims' flesh.

195 Melrose Avenue, Willesden, where Nilsen incinerated the remains of twelve victims in the garden

Police under covers search the garden at Melrose Avenue
for bone fragments

The tarpaulin-covered garden at Melrose Avenue, where
police searched in the snow for human remains

Opposite and above: Dennis Nilsen at Highgate
Magistrates' Court

Fred West as a child

The cellar at 25 Cromwell Street, where Fred West buried six victims

Fred and Rose West, a couple with terrible secrets

Looking over 25 Cromwell Street, Gloucester, as police excavate the garden under cover of tarpaulins

Removing boxed human remains from 25 Cromwell Street

Fred West taken away from Gloucester Magistrates' Court in handcuffs

Rosemary West leaves court after a remand hearing

Pathologist Sir Bernard Spilsbury (in apron) works at the second Crumbles murder site, on the case which inspired him to devise Scotland Yard's "murder bag"

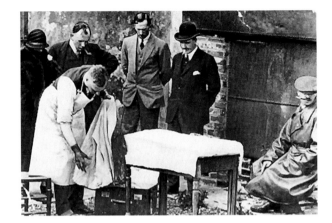

Sir Bernard Spilsbury, the most famous of all pathologists

Ballistics expert Robert Churchill, whose
microscopic examinations could link bullets to
the guns that fired them

Francis Camps, the ebullient pathologist who wrote about his findings in the Christie case

Dr Ronald Teare, the pathologist whose report on Beryl Evans' body was approved by his colleagues five years later

He accepted an invitation to come back for a drink; accepted that it would have to be orange juice as Nilsen was out of vodka, but was a bit surprised to be given his glass in the hall while Nilsen disappeared back into his flat. As Coles desperately wanted a pee more than a drink, he nipped out to the back of the house to urinate against the wall. As he did so, Nilsen appeared, livid with rage. He ranted at him, drove him off the premises and never spoke to him again, but looked daggers at him if they passed in the street.

"Douglas Stewart" appeared on a list of names the SoCOs found in Melrose Avenue which detectives thought might be Nilsen's murder list. When they traced Stewart through his brother and mother, they found that this tough Scot, by this time living in a caravan in Thurso, was yet another who had made a formal complaint to them. In 1980 Stewart was working in a small London hotel, and frequenting the Golden Lion in Dean Street, Soho, more for its Scottish than its homosexual ambience. "Desi" Nilsen, slim, 5 feet 11 inches tall, with straight black hair and glasses, was both gay and a highlander; he was also a chef. He and Stewart got into conversation about the difference between dishes prepared *chausseur* and *forestière* in classical French cuisine. Afterward they went to Nilsen's home, where Stewart dozed off and woke up to find his ankles tied to the chair legs and his host trying to strangle him. He managed to scratch Nilsen's face, and as he withdrew, knocked him down. When he left the flat he dialled 999 from the nearest phone box and a panda car arrived to take his statement. But he smelt of beer, and Nilsen was evidently respectable and convincing when he described a homosexual lovers' quarrel. No action was taken.

Carl Stotter and Paul Nobbs did not complain about Nilsen's murderous assaults on them, as neither could remember them clearly in the morning. Nobbs, a quiet graduate student, woke after a night in Nilsen's flat with frightfully bloodshot eyes and a sore throat. When he went to a doctor he was astounded to be told that somebody had tried to kill him. But as he couldn't remember it, he did nothing until Nilsen's arrest sent the police looking for Paul, the student who got away.

Carl's story was the same in outline. He had been offered a sleeping bag at Melrose Avenue, with a warning that the zip tended to catch. In the night he woke to find the zip strangling him and Nilsen's hands on it. He passed out, and came round to find himself in a bath of cold water, with Nilsen pushing him under. After passing out again, he revived to find himself lying in Nilsen's bed with Nilsen anxiously tending him. Nilsen told Carl he had started to choke in the caught zip, and that he had immersed him in the bath of water to bring him round. Carl doubted this, but did not imagine that he would have a chance of persuading anyone he had been assaulted if it came to his young and disreputable word against this older executive officer of the civil service. After Nilsen's arrest, the search for "Blondie" (as Nilsen called him) who got away, began when Nilsen confessed the episode. He revealed that when he thought he had drowned Stotter, his dog Bleep started licking the body, which showed him that the lad must still be alive. So he went into reverse, and the murderer became the saviour.

Nilsen's confessions still left the question, why? He was not collecting inert bodies as the only way he could find sexual release. He was not robbing his victims. He was not overtly trolling for men to murder: 10 casual visitors had passed through his flats for every one he killed. He was not a man with a frustrating and unsatisfying dead-end job: he had been an army chef for 10 years, then served a year as a probationary Metropolitan policeman, resigning from the force as pay and prospects were in one of their periodic troughs. He would happily have gone on being a bobby if these things had improved. Instead he joined the civil service as a clerical officer at the Denmark Street Job Centre, in Soho, later rising to executive grade and transferring to Kentish Town. Nilsen himself noted that he usually only killed when he was drunk and listening to music with a companion. Survivors commented on his capacity to down huge tumblers of vodka. Peter Jay thinks he was not an alcoholic, but a drunk.

Nilsen was to receive more detailed psychological study than any other English serial killer. Brian Masters, a serious writer specializing in French literature, noticed with interest that Nilsen was carrying a copy of Shakespeare's collected works as he was taken to court. This intrigued him, and, quite unaware of the usual restrictions on prisoners meeting with writers, he wrote to him and was rewarded with a Visitor's Order and an invitation to meet Nilsen in prison. Despite some mildly apoplectic responses in parts of the Home Office and the Lord Chancellor's Office, the deed had been done. Masters was the recognized "friend" of a prisoner whose family were hardly in contact with him. And so, for the first time, a British serial killer was in the process of giving the interviews for an "authorized" biography.

In 1992 came further exposure. Some old video footage Nilsen took of himself indulging in a drunken tirade had already been shown on television, arousing some questions about the propriety of giving such exposure to a convicted serial murderer. There would be even more questions when Mike Morley of Central Television won permission to interview and film Nilsen to add to a series of interviews with American serial killers he had already made. And to do the questioning he took with him Professor Paul Britton, who had become one of the two most prominent psychological profilers in Britain over the previous five years.

There can be little doubt that all this exposure suited Nilsen admirably. Every examination of him has revealed three central features of his personality. Although he is convinced that he is a most unusual person, he is banally ordinary. Although he appears to have a wide range of interests compared with most other serial killers, he is in fact fascinated with himself to the exclusion of almost every-thing else. And, as a commonplace man with inordinate egotism and narcissism, he is an absolutely crashing bore. Featuring in books and studies and appearing on television has given him the opportunity to hold forth to an invisible but, he may assume, cap-tive audience on his favourite topics: himself and his opinions about any subject he cares to discuss.

"Dennis Nilsen is frighteningly normal in the context of what he has done," says Jay. "He is a very ordinary sort of man except when you talk to him. He does quickly become pretty boring if you talk to him about the sort of things he wants to talk about."

"As a person," Masters says, "he, in fact … is not very interesting at all." He admits that: "He can be very interesting in conversation for the first 10 minutes. And then he rapidly becomes rather boring because … you see that his conversation is self-oriented all the time: that he doesn't listen to what other people are saying. He's not interested in an exchange of ideas. He has very clear ideas himself, and they're articulately put. But they're his, and there's nothing else. Nothing else exists. So people tend to walk away from him. And I would have too. I would not have liked him."

This is the most positive objective account anyone has ever felt able to give of Nilsen. For 10 years the relationship with Masters was as near as Nilsen came to having a normal friend to make con-tacts with the outside world for him. The ordinariness of Nilsen's personality and demeanour, contrasting with the horror of his deeds, proved the most unsettling thing about him to Mike Morley. Nilsen himself seems aware that he easily comes over as banal. He demanded explicitly that, however Morley filmed him, he must be made to look interesting. Paul Britton noted that his social skills were underdeveloped, though some of his fantasies were florid. Both men were treated to a conversation manipulator who brought everything back to himself all the time, even hinting that his own home-video efforts showed him to be on a footing with the TV crew. Britton the psychologist and Morley, the seeker after revealing moments of self-exposure for broadcasting, could utilize the self-regarding monologue style of Nilsen's conversation. But it would obviously be unbearable to try to live with, and prompts the Nilsenesque joke that it's a wonder his victims didn't strangle him.

Jay and Masters were both a little surprised by Nilsen's frequent use of black humour, whereby he often tastelessly added to the embarrassment people felt in discussing his offences with him. When he said, "The victim is the dirty platter after the feast and the washing-up is a clinically ordinary task," he may have felt he was the Oscar Wilde of murderers. (He likes quoting Wilde.) When he said, "End of day, end of drinking, end of person," he may have deluded himself that he was matching an American one-line wisecracker like Bob Hope. When he told Masters that any film of his life should list the cast "in order of disappearance", Masters' courtesy hid the fact that he found this jest "abject" and "disgraceful".

Masters, who knows Nilsen better than anyone else, has also described his "illusion" that he is an interesting person in his own right. The volume of Shakespeare that attracted the writer's notice in the first place was supplemented by Nilsen's taste for banal romantic novels by the likes of Barbara Cartland. The endless writing and drawing which makes Nilsen look unusually creative among serial killers would not give him high standing in the ranks of Sunday painters or library literature circles.

Nilsen's absorption with himself led him to ask the police to explain to him why he had committed all these murders, blissfully unaware that his subjective motives were far less important and interesting to them than the concrete facts on which the courts could convict him and put him behind bars. He told Masters that "the burden" of explaining his life had now passed to the biographer. The notion of other people having lives and priorities of their own that outweigh their interest in him is quite foreign to Nilsen. He seems to have had little gratitude for Masters' overcoming his revulsion at his actions and acknowledging some indebtedness for the material which went into the book that made him nationally known. Masters continued to visit Nilsen regularly and communicate with his family for him, but after 10 years Nilsen simply dropped him, probably because he had created a circle of ignorant yes-men in prison who were easier to impress.

Masters' work, like that of others who have studied Nilsen, provides an interesting basis for picking out some general and common features of serial killers. Nilsen's childhood was mildly dysfunctional. His Norwegian father left his mother very soon after he was born, and Nilsen himself suspected his mother of "playing around", so that he might not be Olaf Nilsen's son. Ian Brady, David Berkowitz ("Son of Sam"), Ted Bundy and Charles Manson are just four other serial killers who, with better reason, were never sure who their real fathers were. When, years later, Nilsen found out that his father had changed his surname to Mokesheim (a maternal-line family name), he was further confused, and started using the new name to sign his literary creations.

Nilsen's mother has said that she found it very difficult to cuddle the baby Dennis. Whatever the reason, this gave him a very bad start in life, making it possible for him to have difficulty in bonding with her and forming affectionate attachments to others. He has, indeed, said that he does not love her. She evidently does still love him, and has been hurt by his unreliability in keeping contact with his family. Given his damaged personality, Nilsen should probably be given some credit for always having tried to maintain a surface of proper formal relations with them, although a rather silly quarrel with his older brother Olaf led to a complete break in adult life.

He felt overshadowed by Olaf, and in competition for affection with his younger sister, Sylvia. When he was a child he used to explore and play with his siblings' genitals while they were sleeping: conduct reminiscent of Rose West, who, as a child, found satisfaction in masturbating her little brother. Nilsen believed that his brother at least was aware of this and enjoyed it. He has wondered whether this might have led him to enjoy playing with his victims' inert bodies, which he often bathed, powdered and partially dressed in clean clothing to keep with him for some days.

Like Christie, he was unwilling to confess his sexual nature until he was in company which would evidently accept it. He told the police he supposed he was best described as homosexual, implying falsely that he was not sexually active and denying that he used his victims' bodies for sexual purposes. He admitted his homosexuality to Masters, but told him that after a failure to penetrate the body of his first victim, he did not use them sexually. Robert Ressler forthrightly characterizes this as "a total cop-out. Everything he did would clearly indicate that there was a sexual motivation in doing what he did." But the "cop-out" again makes Nilsen commonplace rather than interesting: many serial killers have difficulty in acknowledging their sexuality, since its very inadequacy lies at the heart of their pathology.

Roy Hazelwood, too, sees Nilsen's crimes as sexually motivated, whether there was sexual activity or not. Nor does he think there is anything mysterious or interesting about Nilsen's letting nine out of 10 visitors leave his flat unscathed. All of us sometimes do and often don't feel like doing certain things.

In fact, as Nilsen admitted to Morley and Britton, there was quite a lot of sexual activity with and around his victims. He satisfied himself on Ken Ockenden's body by friction between the thighs. He masturbated over others. The rich fantasy life observed by Britton had always contained immature sexual components that recall those of other serial killers. Like narcissistic Ian Brady, he played with mirrors during his adolescent masturbation. Sometimes he liked to place himself so that his head was out of vision and he could imagine the hands he saw were someone else's. Sometimes he powdered himself and lay down as if he were a corpse. Notoriously, he attributed his fascination with death to seeing his beloved fisherman grandfather laid out for his wake when he had not been told he had been drowned, and had death described to him as simply "going to a better place".

Ressler explodes with indignation at this excuse, calling it "about as ridiculous as anything I've ever heard". He thinks Nilsen, in common with many other serial killers, is finding something "to sell as a justification for his behaviour. It doesn't wash." (In fairness to Nilsen he seems rather to have trailed his coat with this story, letting others suggest that the childhood trauma was a cause of his adult behaviour.)

More youthful conduct that matches that of his horrible peers includes cruelty to animals: he once hanged a cat to see how long it would take to die, as Brady in Glasgow used to kill cats slowly and observe them. Like Christie and Berkowitz, he enjoyed uniforms. One of the two men with whom he failed to establish a lasting cohabiting relationship recalls him as sharing Brady's interest in Nietzsche and Nazism, at least for a time. (Subsequently his leaning to authority led him to become an active union official in the Civil and Public Services Association.) He joined the Boys' Brigade and the army cadets before letting his love of uniforms lead him into the army, though he compromised with his artistic abilities in deciding to become a chef. It is not surprising that he specialized in visual ornaments and garnishes, decorating salmon in aspic or roast pig with lemon in the mouth and parsley round the ears. He is maligned, however, when it is suggested that there was something sinister about his possessing a set of butcher's knives and a steel wrapped in oilcloth. The fact that most of his colleagues in the Army Catering Corps did not keep such personal equipment marks them down as cooks rather than serious chefs. Nilsen's slightly narrow social skills are probably well indicated by the presence of no fewer than four fellow caterers among the known casual visitors to his flat.

Inadequate social skills again appear in the awkward discovery of his sexual identity during adolescence. Like Dr Harold Shipman, he was unable to cultivate girlfriends and relied on his sister when he needed a partner to take to dances and social functions.

But saying he was like other serial killers in these respects carries one no further in the search for his driving motive. Masters recognizes the strong element of compulsion in Nilsen, rightly remarking that the term "serial killer" says nothing except that there has been an arithmetical sequence of separate crimes. To distinguish killers like Nilsen and Christie from killers like Smith and Haigh, he proposes the useful term "addictive killer". And Nilsen, with his repeated inability to explain why he did it and his acknowledgment that, on finding himself looking at another body he had strangled, he would become aware of a buzzing in his ears and think, "Uh-oh! Here we go again", is clearly describing an addictive compulsion. The recent American work pointing to a need to control as the common thread makes sense of Nilsen's actions. The great bore who wanted to pontificate about anything and everything, and brush off disagreement with the phrase "We're not on the same wavelength" tried to control his retreating audiences by asking the sympathetic one back to his flat for a drink. Then, wanting him as a partner in bed, but doubting his social skill at seduction, he would kill him. This had the further advantage that he could control his companion's actions and appearance completely for a few days. He could take the body to bed with him. He could put it in a chair and hold its hand, and tell it about his frustrating day at the office. (Virtually every day, interacting with other people entailed some frustration for Nilsen.) His close relationship with Bleep may be seen as a social inadequate's preference for the uncritical admiration of a notoriously emotionally dependent animal. But when his dog died in police custody, Nilsen demonstrated his comparatively affectless nature. Unlike Myra Hindley, who threw a tantrum and called the police "murderers" when Puppet died, Nilsen took it in his stride.

His need to control every situation was shown again in his recurrent changes of legal representation. He sacked his legal-aid solicitor, saying he wanted to defend himself. Then he changed his mind and engaged Ralph Haeems, who had become well known when, as a solicitor's clerk, he acted as a go-between for the Kray twins and their gang members. But then Nilsen switched back to his previous solicitor. All the time he was trying to control and manipulate the situation, as later he would try to control and manipulate writers and interviewers who visited him.

And so, earlier, he tried to control people into being the audience for his dull harangues. He was, as the title of Masters' book famously said, "killing for company".

This explanation wins Ressler's complete approval. Again Nilsen becomes one of a kind, not a unique individual. Ressler compares him to Jeffrey Dahmer of Milwaukee (a similarity Masters noted, too) and Bob Berdella of Kansas City. Dahmer makes the situation almost blatantly explicit. His first murder took place when he was 18, abandoned on his own by his separated parents, who took his little brother away, and left Jeffrey in the family home with a wonky fridge full of food and a battered car. When a strange lad from whom he hitched a lift came in for a beer and then proposed to go home, Dahmer couldn't bear being left on his own any longer. So he killed him.

Roy Hazelwood finds Dahmer unique. "I don't think there's ever been anyone like Jeffrey Dahmer," he says. And certainly Nilsen never did anything as crazy as Dahmer did when, in Ressler's words, "he desired to keep his victims alive by drilling holes in their heads and injecting acid into their brains to kill their intellects and keep their bodies alive, to keep them as sex zombies. Which is not," says Ressler, a little obviously, "a rational thing to do."

But Hazelwood does not underrate the likelihood that Nilsen revealed an unusual truth about himself. "We don't expect to hear something like 'I killed for company,'" he remarks. "It's so aberrant that I find it hard to believe he would have made that up."

Did even Masters "make up" the phrase which seems to define Nilsen? DCI Jay was impressed by the aura of evil surrounding Nilsen and his flat. He was misled by Nilsen's deliberate trail of confusion about his own homosexuality. But it seems that it was he who came up with the homely phrase that put the crimes in perspective. "I think he killed for company," says Jay, "and that's what I told Brian Masters I thought had happened. There was no logical reason why he killed. It wasn't for money. It wasn't for sexual reasons. It wasn't jealousy, it wasn't hate, it wasn't any of the usual reasons. It was just some bizarre idea that he had to end an individual's life then and there."

And that, in the end, is the only thing of any interest about Dennis Nilsen.

FROM NILSEN TO
THE WESTS

THE DECADE BETWEEN Dennis Nilsen's conviction and Fred West's arrest saw two of the most highly publicized developments in criminal detection since fingerprinting. And in England, clinical psychologist Paul Britton was intimately involved with both developments.

Detective Superintendent David Baker of Leicester CID was responsible for the earliest successes of both the techniques. When the 1984 murder of dog groomer Caroline Osborne showed psychologically interesting features – her hands bound with twine, and a piece of paper with a pentagram left near the body – he contacted Britton, whose work on a girl's embarrassing infatuation with a policeman had made a good impression. The police believed from witness testimony that their man was very tall and dressed in drab combat fatigues at the time of the murder. The puzzle fascinated Britton, who had never before thought of combining psychologically perceived patterns with criminal investigation. He advised the police that their man would be physically strong, be interested in knives and would keep satanic and violent pornography to feed his fantasies. The following year a nurse called Amanda Weedon was killed, and her stab wounds suggested that the same man was responsible.

When a young man called Paul Bostock arrived at the police station, on his grandmother's advice, to clear himself, the police realized that he fitted both their and Paul Britton's descriptions. Britton now advised them on the most productive ways of interviewing him, and the result was a confession. Although the term was not generally used in Britain at the time, this was the first successful use of psychological profiling in the UK.

In 1985 Paul Britton became head of the Regional Forensic Psychology Service in Leicestershire, which brought him into the picture very quickly the following year when the police arrested a young kitchen porter for the murder of a schoolgirl in a lane running beside Carlton Hayes Hospital. This was the second time a schoolgirl had been murdered in lanes alongside Britton's former workplace: the first, in 1983, remained unsolved.

The kitchen porter matched descriptions of a man seen in the vicinity of the second murder; he had told friends that the girl's body lay in the lane before it was discovered, and his responses to interviewing revealed knowledge of the murder which had never been published. His statements veered unstably between confessing and withdrawing his confessions. He had previous convictions for indecent assaults. The police had little doubt they had the right man, and were only mildly irritated when his father insisted on laboratory tests to establish his innocence.

There was dried semen in the victim's pubic hair, and this was sent to Professor Alec Jeffreys at Leicester University, whose experimental new identification process based on producing visual images of the patterns of DNA in human cells had been used successfully in some immigration cases. The DNA comparison revealed immediately that the semen on the schoolgirl's body had not come from the kitchen porter: it had, however, been deposited by the same man who raped, sodomized and killed the other schoolgirl near the hospital two years earlier. This was a considerable embarrassment to the police, who had charged an innocent man and held him for several months. Paul Britton examined the taped interviews, and confirmed that the police had not unwittingly fed any incriminating answers. It seemed likely that that the kitchen porter had peeped on the second murder from a hidden vantage point. The real problem was that a killer who had already struck twice was still at large.

Britton advised the police that their man was probably either married or in a relationship, since he had been sufficiently sexually satisfied to forgo murderous assaults for three years. He and the police agreed that the killer showed local knowledge. And Britton also added that crimes of this magnitude could not be first offences: the murderer must have some sort of record for indecency.

Superintendent Baker turned to the science which had undermined his first charge. The villages of Narborough, Enderby and Littlethorpe, near the hospital, were small enough for all resident men to be asked for blood samples and saliva swabs for DNA testing. Leicestershire being hunting country, this ambitious experiment was nicknamed "The Blooding".

It seemed at first to have failed. Then a bakery worker told friends that, using a doctored passport for identification, he had taken the test on behalf of a colleague. His manager reported this to the police. The man was arrested and charged with conspiracy to pervert the course of justice. His colleague, Colin Pitchfork, was hauled in and confessed immediately.

Although he matched Britton's profile – married, with a conviction for indecent exposure – this case achieved fame as the pioneering DNA identification case, and Britton's role went more or less unremarked at the time. It was Professor David Canter, then at Surrey University, who first attracted public attention as an English profiler. In 1985 he was invited to lunch at Scotland Yard with Detective Superintendent Thelma Wagner and Detective Chief Inspector John Grieve, who had met an ex-student of Canter's and learned of his general awareness of the new American art of psychological profiling. Following their conversation, Canter contacted the police when he read an *Evening Standard* account of the search for the "Railway Rapists", who, since 1982, had committed 24 assaults near overground railway stations in and around the perimeter of London. In 15 assaults they apparently worked as a pair, in nine one apparently worked on his own. It seemed to Canter that this problem would lend itself to the profiling approach, and he was invited to assist the Operation Hart team which combined units from the Met, Surrey Constabulary and the South Eastern Regional Crime Squad to investigate the rapes and three 1986 murders which appeared to be the work of the solo rapist. Canter, who always acknowledges indebtedness to other researchers and investigators, was familiar with the scholarly papers published in learned journals by members of the FBI Behavioral Science Unit, but now realized they had never given an account of their profiling methods. So as an environmental scientist, he started by examining the time and place sequence of the assaults and murders, deducing immediately that the killer-rapist lived somewhere in Kensal Green in a "comfort zone" bounded by the first three crimes.

Whereas Britton has the creative imagination of an artist, and ponders problems until patterns of truth appear in his mind, Canter is the sort of psychologist who would like his science to be "harder" and more statistical. He turned rapidly to the computer as the most accurate and logical way of assessing disparate pieces of information. With Detective Constable Rupert Heritage, who was to become one of his closest associates, he started databasing a judicious mix of FBI-tested psychological probabilities – the rapist talked confidently as he approached his victims, so he was or had been married or in a relationship; he must have previous form for milder sexual offences; his skills in trying to cover his tracks showed that he was, in Ressler's terms, "organized", and not very young and inexperienced; his willingness to abuse and murder a 15-year-old suggested a childless man who had never bonded with progeny of his own – with practical "clues" observed in the case – the perpetrator's familiarity with the overground railway system; his use of an unusual string made from paper for binding victims, and an unusual thumb-tie familiar to martial-arts enthusiasts. The computer instantly popped up the name of John Duffy, previously lying at about number 1,500 of the 2,000 suspects. The police had discounted his previous sexual offence since it was committed against his estranged wife and had been categorized as a domestic dispute. Duffy was convicted of two of the three murders and Canter's name was made. Fourteen years later he confessed to the third, saying that, as the police had long suspected, his rape accomplice, David Mulcahy, was equally complicit in the murders. Mulcahy was tried and convicted in 2001.

With becoming modesty Canter has always suggested that he enjoyed luck as well as judgement. He failed to make the right deductions about the Duffy's employment history. He would not have made the point about childlessness had he been aware of Colin Pitchfork, married, a father and well on the way to becoming a sexual serial killer of teenage girls. (Nobody would be likely to make such a deduction again after Fred West's exposure in 1992.) But the computer had proved its worth. A repeat of the Yorkshire Ripper scandal had been avoided.

Canter and Heritage then visited the FBI Academy at Quantico, and discovered that the great masters of psychological profiling (now usually called Criminal Investigation Analysis) came to rapid, intuitive, hunch-like conclusions based on their wide experience, and then rationalized them. This encouraged him to develop a remarkable project for breaking down fragments of observation into computer-storable data, so that the computer could offer up suspect profiles and match them to known previous offenders' or current suspects' characteristics.

Neither psychological profiling nor DNA identification was well known until the end of the decade, however. In the meantime two nasty London serial killers attracted headlines. Michele de Marco Lupo, an upmarket sadomasochistic rent boy with an international clientele, killed a number of casual sexual partners picked up in gay pubs. They were not usually anonymous drifters like Nilsen's victims, and Lupo was caught when one escaped and led the police on a traditional plod-and-question tour of gay pubs. It seems possible that the AIDS which ultimately killed Lupo in prison triggered the rage which led him to murder.

Kenneth Erskine, the "Stockwell Strangler", seemed both half-witted and cunning in the sequence of break-ins in which he robbed, sodomized and killed a number of old ladies and gentlemen. Classically "disorganized", he left fingerprints and clues to his identity all over the place, and let himself be seen and his voice be heard by survivors. When he came to trial, he had to be prevented from masturbating in court. Yet the police have never been able to trace the squat or squats where he hid out while using a number of different National Insurance cards to make fraudulent collections of giro cheques.

Joseph Wambaugh's book *The Blooding* and the film of *The Silence of the Lambs* made the new techniques internationally famous. But neither contributed to solving the case which broke in 1992, eliciting more intensely distressing sympathy for cruelly abused children than anything since the Moors Murders, and demonstrating some new refinements of forensic pathology and odontology — the study of teeth and dental records for courtroom purposes. Number 25 Cromwell Street, Gloucester, proved a worse House of Horrors than 10 Rillington Place. And while Fred West was universally recognized as a devastatingly frightening murderer, his sadistic wife Rose would find a strange defender in Brian Masters.

FRED AND ROSEMARY WEST

IN AUGUST 1992 Gloucestershire Police began investigating an accusation of child abuse levelled against a builder and his wife. Fred West was charged with raping a minor and his wife, Rose, was charged with assisting him. The case fell through because the two children on whose testimony it depended refused, in the end, to give evidence. But Fred and Rose West lost custody of their youngest children as police and social workers uncovered more and more of the bizarre sexual activities in their home at 25 Cromwell Street, Gloucester. Parts of the house were equipped like a brothel, with sex toys, pornographic videos and the like. Fred evidently had no objection to Rose's having sexual relations with other people, and Rose had advertised in contact magazines and prostituted herself.

While the children were in care another accusation came to light: one of murder. Apparently their parents had threatened them that they would end up buried "under the patio", "like Heather". This information was passed to the police, and they began their search in the garden of 25 Cromwell Street.

Heather, it seemed, was the children's elder sister. She hadn't been seen for seven years. Her parents said she had left home when she was 16, as soon as she finished her schooling. There had been an argument with her father and she walked out. They weren't worried about her. They were glad to see her go. It was what the family wanted.

There was already a court case on file proving that Fred and Rose had been jointly involved in a vicious sexual assault on a young woman. Caroline Raine was 16 in September 1972 when she was hitch-hiking home from Tewkesbury to Cinderford and accepted a lift from a couple in a grey Ford Popular. Rose West was herself only 18 at the time; Fred was 30. They told Caroline they were from Gloucester, and wanted a nanny to look after their children. It had long been Caroline's dream to be a children's nanny, and very soon she moved in to 25 Cromwell Street to help with eight-year-old Anna-Marie, two-year-old Heather and the baby, May June (whose name was soon changed to Mae). She soon moved out again. Fred's unseemly boasting and uncalled-for offer to perform an abortion for her if she should ever need it "just rang alarm bells" in her head.

But in December she was once again seeking a lift home from her usual hitch-hiking spot outside a pub in Tewkesbury when the Wests' Ford pulled up. Rose got out, all smiles, and said, "Oh, Caroline, we've missed you!" Fred leaned over to the passenger window and said, "I'm sorry if I've upset you. I didn't mean to upset you. But we've missed you and the kids have missed you. Would you like to come back?"

Caroline didn't want to make a fuss, so she got into the back of the car. But she was quite unprepared for Fred looking at her in the mirror as he drove away, and saying to Rose, "Have a feel, Rose. See if she's had sex."

"Get off! I want to get out," cried Caroline. "Pull up!"

Fred pulled up at the roadside. But instead of letting Caroline out he started punching her head. Caroline passed out, and when she came to, Fred was tying her hands behind her back, and then gagging her with strong adhesive tape passed around her head. She was driven to Cromwell Street, and submitted to hours of sexual abuse and torture. The Wests began with what Caroline could only describe as "a genital examination". She was frightened and crying, not knowing what they were going to do next. They blindfolded her, and then, while Rose held her legs apart, Fred flogged her genitals with his belt. After a while they tied her to a chair and went downstairs to make a cup of tea. For the next four hours they continued the bizarre alternation of sexually abusing and tormenting Caroline, and then, during inexplicable intermissions, giving her cups of tea and behaving like a nice, friendly couple.

At seven o'clock in the morning there was a ring at the doorbell. Fred went downstairs to see who it was, and Caroline started shouting for help. Rose panicked, covered her face with a pillow and leaned on it. When Fred came back he was in a rage. He snatched the pillow away and snarled at Caroline, "You stupid bitch! You shouldn't have done that! We're gonna have to kill you now!" His threats seemed to parallel something that would emerge over 20 years later, for he said, "We're going to keep you in the cellar and when we've finished with you we're gonna kill you and bury you under the paving stones of Gloucester."

But when Rose left the room Fred's manner changed. He took his trousers off and raped Caroline, but when he had finished, he said, "I shouldn't have done that. You're here for Rose's pleasure, and I shouldn't have touched you … She's gonna be really angry if she knows." Caroline took this opportunity to suggest that if he let her go, she would promise not to tell anyone what had happened, and Fred agreed to this. She very sensibly ignored her promise once she was free, and told the police all about this terrifying couple. Faced with a possible rape charge, the Wests decided to plead guilty to indecent assault and actual bodily harm. Then, it was explained to Caroline, if she dropped the accusation of rape she would not have to appear in court. She was warned that otherwise she would be put through humiliating cross-examination by the Wests' counsel. Understandably she decided she would rather stay right away from the proceedings and let the guilty pleas run their course. So it was that Fred and Rose received mild sentences of £25 fines for each of the offences they admitted: a grand total of £100.

"That's what I'm worth. I'm worthless," thought Caroline. But 22 years later the rest of the world wondered how this terrible pair could have got away with such a light slap on the wrists for submitting a teenage girl to 12 hours of abominable pain and mortification. The authorities who heard the West children's story over two decades later wondered still more about a sinister echo.

"We're gonna kill you and bury you under the paving stones of Gloucester ..."

"... buried under the patio like Heather ..."

Could it be that the Wests had gone beyond bizarre and cruel sex practices to murder? Could their own child be lying under the slabs of the patio that Fred had laid to cover much of the 60-foot garden behind his house?

On February 24, 1994 the police arrived at 25 Cromwell Street determined to find out. They brought a small mechanical digger with them. When Fred came home from work he had only to look out of his window to see that they meant business. The following day he confessed to killing his daughter Heather. When Rose heard of Fred's confession she reacted with violent emotion. Some observers felt this was genuine and initiated her complete estrangement from her husband. Others thought it was an act.

As the patio slabs were being removed, a bone was discovered near the back door. Pathologist Professor Bernard Knight was called in to determine whether it was human. It was, he said. It was also female. And, when digging in the garden unearthed more bones, he was able to say that they had found somebody's skeleton. But also, as he remarked to Detective Superintendent John Bennett, the Senior Investigating Officer, "Well, either she's got three legs, or you've got another body!"

And as Fred was being led to the magistrates' court for the first hearing of the charge that he had killed Heather, he admitted that the garden contained other bodies, also victims of his. There was Shirley Robinson, who was a friend of Heather, he said, and another girl who was a friend of Shirley. In each case he claimed to have got into an argument with the girl, lost his temper and realized too late that he had killed them.

But he did not mention that Shirley Robinson had been six months pregnant when she died, nor that those friends and neighbours who knew of the pregnancy were also sure that the child was his and that Rose knew it. The foetal skeleton was found with its mother's. The body of the third girl in the garden turned out to be that of Alison Chambers, who had disappeared in August 1979 after living in a care home near Cromwell Street. It became clear that she had come into Fred's life too close to the time of Shirley's disappearance to have been the girl's longstanding friend. The police realized that the grinning and apparently cooperative man they were interrogating, who seemed to answer all their questions so reliably, was not to be trusted at all. He told them just what suited him or what he felt sure they were going to find out in any case.

Since they were trying to extract the truth from a serial killer whose psychological make-up required them to treat his answers with caution, the police called in an expert. They wanted to know when Fred started on his career of murder. And they wanted to know whether Rose had been with him at the time. The forensic psychologist Dr Paul Britton, who had worked with Superintendent Bennett on previous cases, came and looked at the case history, and then reported back to the police. The three bodies in the garden would not be the only women Fred had killed, he warned them. Britton discerned that Fred and Rose showed a pattern of "combined depravity". They were mutually supportive sadistic predators, equally involved in atrocities. The other victims might be found anywhere Fred had lived, and anywhere he had worked. To start with, having finished in the garden of 25 Cromwell Street, the police must search the house. They would have to take apart every inch of it, for they would certainly find more bodies there. "He used the garden because the house is full," Britton told them.

The police embarked on the search. Everything was photographed and filmed. The floorboards were taken up. The walls were X-rayed. But before this search was near completion a member of the public contacted the incident room with a missing-person report that seemed to point to the Wests. Lynda Gough, a 19-year-old, had disappeared in 1973 after moving into the Wests' home when they befriended her. She had left a note for her parents simply saying that she had found a flat and they would be hearing from her. When they didn't, Mrs Gough went to Lynda's workplace and learned that she had been staying at 25 Cromwell Street. She then visited the house, and Rose answered the door wearing a cardigan that Mrs Gough believed she recognized as her Lynda's. She also thought she saw other clothing that belonged to her daughter hanging on the Wests' washing line. Fred and Rose told Mrs Gough that Lynda had moved on. But she was never seen again.

This report was very significant to the police, for it involved Rose. She had apparently been wearing Lynda's cardigan; she had been supporting a story of Fred's that might well be a cover for one of his murders. Asked about Lynda Gough, Fred realized that further investigation of her disappearance might implicate Rose, and his wife was so important to him that he declined to be interviewed further for the time being.

Yet for some reason he changed his mind later the same day and sent his solicitor with a signed note for Superintendent Bennett, confessing to nine murders, including Lynda Gough's. Her body was found underneath a bathroom that Fred had constructed where a garage had previously been attached to the house. Fred was charged with her murder and so was Rose. Although in his confession Fred tried to exonerate his wife, the police now had separate evidence against her.

The other bodies were, as Britton had predicted, inside the house. Fred had buried them in small square pits in the cellar, which was later converted into a nursery bedroom for the children. The beds covered the graves of five young women, now reduced to skeletalized remains. An unusual number of bones were missing from the graves, particularly from the hands and feet. Other things found in the graves suggested that the victims had been tied up and gagged. Fred was taken back to the house and tried to help the police by chalking squares on the cellar floor at the points where he believed he had interred his victims. As in Dennis Nilsen's case, the problem for the police now was to identify them.

Yet another problem was the hunt for further victims. Britton had explicitly advised that the search should cover all the places where Fred had lived and worked. The police wanted to know just how early Fred had taken up the practice of murder and whether he was already a killer before he met Rose. To this end they appealed for anyone who had known the Wests for any reason at all over the previous 25 years to come forward. They were particularly interested in tracing Fred's first wife, Catherine "Rena" Costello, and her daughter Charmaine. Rena and Fred had married in 1962 when Fred was 21 and Rena 18. At the time of their marriage Rena was pregnant by another man, and in March 1963 Charmaine was born. The following year Fred and Rena had a daughter of their own.

They led an up-and-down life over the next three years as Fred held a succession of jobs, and he moved alone to a caravan site near Gloucester in December 1965. Rena joined him in February 1966. From time to time they quarrelled and separated. And finally, in 1969, Rena abandoned Fred for good, leaving him to care for the two girls, with the help of the social services.

In 1971 Rena came back to Gloucester looking for her daughters. By this time Fred was living with Rose. Rena's visit to Fred proved to be the last time anyone could confirm seeing her. In 1994 Fred confessed that this was because he had killed her.

He had buried Rena's body, he told the police, in a field near his native village of Much Marcle, just over the Gloucestershire border in Herefordshire. This presented the enquiry with a massive logistical problem. A field was a much larger area to excavate than a house and garden, and even though Fred said where he thought the body lay, it took a month's work, with earth-moving equipment displacing thousands of tons of soil, and nine officers digging a four-foot deep trench along the hedgerow, before Rena's remains were found. Fred was promptly charged with her murder.

At this point he set the police a new task. He told them he thought there was another woman's body buried in the next field, although he denied having anything to do with killing her. The denial might be worth little, but the further search seemed necessary. As they embarked on renewed digging, Fred, during the hundreds of hours of taped interviews the police conducted with him, revealed that a former girlfriend of his, Anna McFall, known as Annie, had somehow died, and it seemed it was her body that was being sought. The body had been dismembered before being stuffed upright into its narrow square grave: a "signature" means of disposing of his victims, already noted in Cromwell Street.

Annie had been a friend of Rena in Glasgow. When Fred and Rena went south in 1965, Annie went with them. Although originally company for Rena, she ultimately found herself living with Fred as the first West marriage bumped and banged along its roller-coaster course. The police were confident that Fred was the father of the child she was carrying when she died, and they charged him with her murder. So one of their questions was now answered to their satisfaction. Fred West was a murderer before he married Rose. Annie McFall had been lying in the field since 1967, two years before Fred met Rose.

Frederick West and Rosemary Letts met in 1969 when he was 28 and she was 15. As Brian Masters (who later interviewed her for a book he was writing) has observed, Rose was a pretty and giggly young girl, not at all obviously like the dowdy and depressed house-wife whom the world saw being taken to court in 1995. Moreover, photographs of Fred and Rose and family photographs taken during the years of their marriage show closeness, affection and happiness on their faces. The police and Paul Britton, however, put a sinister interpretation on this couple's inseparable unity. It was the bond between two people who found enjoyment and satisfaction in the dreadful things that went on in 25 Cromwell Street and that only they knew about.

What about the house where they had lived previously? Another number 25, in Midland Road, Gloucester, it held the ground-floor flat where, at just 17 years of age, young Rosemary had to look after Fred's stepdaughter Charmaine, his real daughter Anna-Marie, and her own daughter Heather, while Fred served a short prison sentence in 1970–71 for the petty thieving from his employers and building sites which was his unbreakable lifelong habit. And while Rose lived in Midland Road, Charmaine (eight years old in 1971) disappeared. Gone back to live with her mother, Fred and Rose told the neighbours. Continuing her schooling somewhere else. But Fred's long, rambling statements now admitted that this was untrue. Charmaine was buried at Midland Road, under a cellar area adjacent to an extension. Since Fred himself had laid the foundations in which Charmaine was buried, there could be no doubt about his involvement in disposing of the body.

But could he actually have killed her? The police doubted it. Charmaine had disappeared in June 1971. Fred had been in prison until the 24th of that month. Could it be that Rose had become a murderess when just 17 and trying to fit into the role of mother to one, stepmother to two? Possibly. Some observers were becoming increasingly convinced that Rose's sadistic sexual awakening by Fred had uncovered a more dominant and violent personality than his, and a more relentless sexual appetite. The FBI's Robert Ressler calls them "a perfect union of two totally deviant – you know, degenerate – people".

The deviance and degeneracy moved – with the Wests – to Cromwell Street a year later. In December 1972 Caroline Raine had her brush with death. In April 1973 Lynda Gough made her fatal visit to the house. And in November of that year the first of the girls later disinterred from the cellar disappeared. Carol "Caz" Cooper was 15 years old and lived in a care home in Worcester. The weekend after Guy Fawkes' Night she was given a weekend pass to go and stay with her grandmother at the nearby village of Warndon. Before setting off that evening she went to the cinema with her boyfriend, and he saw her on to the 9.15 bus from the centre of Worcester. She never reached her grandmother's house. Nobody knows how Fred West abducted her from such a short bus journey. It has been speculated that he must have met her on some previous occasion, but her family said that this was not the case.

Fred's next victim, 21-year-old Lucy Partington, was in her final year at Exeter University, and hoping to go on to the Courtauld Institute in London to pursue postgraduate studies in medieval art. The daughter of a research scientist and the niece of the novelist Kingsley Amis, Lucy was a recent convert to Roman Catholicism and a young woman of refinement and respectability. It is certain that Fred's later claims to have known her for some time and even to have had a relationship with her were complete lies. How he ever even persuaded her to accept a lift from him remains a mystery. But on 27 December 1973 she was expected to return to her mother's home in Gretton on the last bus from Cheltenham, where she had visited a disabled friend for the day. And that friend was the last person to see her again until her remains were found at 25 Cromwell Street.

The next victim was another student. Thérèse Siegenthaler was Swiss, studying sociology at Woolwich Polytechnic in London. At 21 she was almost exactly a year older than Rose. She was self-reliant, working part time at the Bally shoe shop in the Swiss Centre in Leicester Square and taking judo classes. So she felt well able to take care of herself, financially and physically, as she set off on a hitch-hiking trip to Ireland during the Easter vacation. Theatre tickets booked for the end of April signified her clear intention of returning. But she never reached Ireland, and she never came back. With more of his implausible braggadocio, Fred claimed Thérèse as yet another of his recurrent sexual partners. She was buried in the cellar of 25 Cromwell Street.

The next Cromwell Street cellar victim provided the first hint of a connection with her predecessors. Shirley Hubbard, aged 15 in 1974, lived with foster parents in Droitwich, and worked in the make-up department of Debenhams in Worcester. The fourteenth of November was the department store's early-closing day, and she spent the afternoon in the town with her boyfriend. At half past nine that evening he put her on the bus for Droitwich. And that was the last time she was seen.

Carol Cooper. Lucy Partington. Shirley Hubbard. Three girls who went for buses; two of whom were seen to board them; all of whom were never seen again. The disappearances might be linked. It was a possible clue. But nobody was able to build a trail from it. In Shirley's case there was no suggestion that she had made her way outside the immediate area of Worcester, or indeed that she had gone to Gloucestershire.

Another victim buried in the cellar actually did have previous connections with 25 Cromwell Street. Juanita Mott, the daughter of an American serviceman and an English mother, was something of a wayward girl. Eighteen years old in April 1975, she already had in her past an ectopic pregnancy and a conviction for stealing a pension book. Also some association with Fred West, to whom she wrote in 1974 and at whose house she may have stayed during that year. In April 1975 she was staying with a friend in Newent, Gloucestershire, whose children she was to babysit on the 12th. The night before, she set out to hitch-hike from Newent to Gloucester, promising to be back the next day. She never came. She was reported missing to the police, but was not seen again until Fred's cellar was dug up.

When these bodies were found, DNA analysis had not reached the point at which such skeletalized remains could be positively identified. It would be necessary to work from the teeth and skulls, if possible. Nor would this be an entirely simple matter. Dental records are not normally retained for 20 years after a patient's death.

However, Dr David Whittaker, a forensic dentist at the University of Wales Medical College, was master of a battery of scientific procedures by which he would be able to confirm the identities of the bodies in the basements. Chromosomes in the tooth pulp could determine the bodies' sex, though this in itself only confirmed the conclusions reached by pathologist Professor Bernard Knight from examining the bones. Amino acids in teeth undergo molecular change at the same rate as the body, and from these it was possible to work out the girls' ages at the times of their deaths. More remarkable still, traces of drugs administered in childhood remained in the teeth, and it was possible to calculate the ages at which they had been taken. Thus, as there was now reasonable knowledge of what medicine was prescribed for what illness, each girl's medical history could be roughly charted. And finally Whittaker asked for as many photographs of the victims as possible, taken as near to the times of their disappearances as possible. With these he would revert to that technique pioneered in the identification of Buck Ruxton's victims. The skulls were carefully photographed from the same distance and angle with similar lenses. The pictures were superimposed. And it was instantly apparent whether or not the skull fitted the face.

The most dramatic discovery of all came when a photograph of Charmaine taken in April 1971 was superimposed on the skull found at 25 Midland Road. Although the eye sockets and jaw line fitted perfectly, Whittaker was able to show where little teeth that had not fully erupted from the gums had grown further. And from that, using formulae familiar to dentists, he was able to calculate just how much older the child was when she died. This evidence would prove of vital importance when Rose finally stood trial for Charmaine's murder.

Before he could be brought to trial, Fred committed suicide in prison. Dr Britton had warned that this might happen. Fred valued Rose more than anything else, including his own life, Britton reckoned. As long as he was able to protect her by making confessions that exonerated her; as long as she accepted this protection, and he enjoyed public attention, Fred would want to live. But once the interrogation sessions were over, the crown's case was prepared and Fred was put on remand away from police interviews and the public's horrified awe, then he might try to kill himself, especially if he felt that Rose had deserted and repudiated him.

Britton's predictions proved accurate. From the time that Fred confessed to Heather's murder, Rose publicly withdrew from him. Once he was alone in prison he started to make statements which no longer exonerated her. And finally, on New Year's Day 1995, Fred West hanged himself.

The prosecution wondered whether they might now fail to get a conviction. Fred's habitual boastfulness had made it a certainty that he would convict himself if he went into the witness box. But Rose was made of stronger stuff, and Britton did not think she was going to confess to anything.

Nor did she. She faced trial alone at Winchester Crown Court in October and November 1995. She was charged with 10 murders – of all the bodies discovered except Anna (Annie) McFall's and Rena Costello West's. She denied everything. But the evidence persuaded the jury to convict her on all counts. Particularly influential, it seemed to observers, were Dr Whittaker's demonstration from Charmaine's teeth that she had died before the end of June 1971 (before Fred West was released from Leyhill Prison), and Caroline Raine's memory of the dreadful things done to her by the older man she always found louche, and the woman of almost her own age who had seemed truly sympathetic and caring until she suddenly grabbed at her private parts in the back of the Ford Popular.

"At least with Fred you knew what you were getting," says Caroline today. "But Rose had been a friend. It's like having your mother turn round and do that to you. I had nightmares ... I thought, I can redeem myself by helping to get Rose convicted. And I put some ghosts to rest."

CONCLUSION

In 1900 JACK THE RIPPER was unique. An evil bogeyman whose like had not been seen before or since. Nobody thought of him as initiating a definable category of murderer, with Neill Cream as the second exemplar.

In 2000 convicted serial rapist Alun Kyte was given a further belated trial, and convicted of two murders that had occurred some six years earlier. He was immediately headlined as "the Midlands Ripper", and a string of murders dating back over the previous two decades were optimistically ascribed to him. The type was defined, expected and confidently categorized, even in a case where the FBI's requisite total of three killings to make a series had not been established.

In any case, hindsight suggests that the equation of three killings to make one serialist was possibly oversimple. There can be little doubt that Colin Pitchfork, the first murderer convicted on DNA identification evidence, and Raymond Morris, the Cannock Chase child molester and murderer, would both have proceeded from two to many more killings had they not been caught in time. Colin Ireland proved that the characteristic narcissism of the serial killer may now become a conscious component of the motive for murder, since serial killers attract so much public attention. Ireland killed five homosexual men between March and June 1993, often visiting the same clubs as Michele De Marco Lupo had frequented in search of victims. He telephoned the police anonymously, taunting them and threatening to kill a new victim every week. And when his tally reached five, he boasted that he was now a serial killer. The peculiar tendency of certain serial killers to inject themselves into the investigation led to his undoing, when closed circuit television pictures of one of the victims walking through Charing Cross station with his killer were made public. Ireland decided to identify himself to the police as the man on the CCTV, hoping to clear himself. But he had left a fingerprint at one crime scene, and had little option but to confess when questioned. CCTV would play its part, again, in identifying the serial bomber David Copeland, who strayed into its picture when leaving his bomb at London's Brixton market in 1999.

The exposure of the Wests had cleared up disappearances going back 20 years. Improvements in scientific and information-recovery techniques meant that such delayed crime-solving was becoming commoner as the twentieth century drew to a close. Robert Black was imprisoned in 1990 for sexual assault on a young girl. At the time the police believed this was a first offence on his part and possibly something of an aberration. Only in 1994 was it noticed that Black's job as a van driver, delivering posters all over Britain, put him in place as the possible murderer of three little girls who had been separately abducted from the Scottish borders and dumped in the Midlands between 1982 and 1986. After Black's conviction for the murders of Susan Maxwell, Caroline Hogg and Sarah Harper, psychologist Ray Wyre interviewed him, and reached the conclusion that Black had probably murdered Genette Tate in south-west England in1978 and even April Fabb in East Anglia, as far back as 1969. And police on the European mainland noted that some unsolved child murders in Amsterdam, Paris and Essen coincided with times when Black had been in those vicinities. It was not an unprecedented occurrence, then, when the addition of Alun Kyte's DNA readings to the national data bank in 1998 popped out the computerized information that this was the hitherto undiscovered man who had left his sperm in the 1994 murder victim Tracy Turner.

In killing prostitutes and girl hitch-hikers, Kyte was reverting to familiar patterns of victim selection. Similarly, Peter Moore, a Welshman who killed four men picked up in homosexual clubs in 1995, was not doing anything exceptional by the standards of previous serial killers. But Dr Harold Shipman, arrested in 1998 and convicted of 15 murders at the beginning of 2000, represented something that seemed new and extraordinary. In the first place the police believed that he was responsible for well over 100 murders, and after his conviction had sufficient evidence to put a further 23 of them before the coroner's court. So "Fred" Shipman is pretty certainly Britain's worst multiple murderer in terms of sheer numbers.

On the other hand, he is certainly not the worst in terms of cruelty. His victims all died peacefully of morphine overdoses, many in their own homes and some in the doctor's office. They had no pain, no fear of death, and the reassuring presence of their trusted GP. Shipman was not motivated by the sadistic wish to see torment and terror in people's eyes that fuelled Fred West. Although he seems to have perpetrated petty thefts of cash and costume jewellery from some of his later victims, and was ultimately caught in a ridiculously amateurish attempt to forge a will, he was not consistently a murderer for gain like George Joseph Smith. Unlike his medical predecessor Neill Cream, he was not obsessed with sex. Lust for or disgust with his patients seems to have played no part in his decision to end their lives. Nor, as a doctor, should he have found life so tedious that he needed the horrible excitement of murder.

Despite the misleading fictional character of Hannibal Lecter, serial killers usually seem to have grimly dull and boring interior lives and jobs, even though they may, like Ed Kremer in America, have remarkably high IQs, or, like Dennis Nilsen and Ted Bundy, the misleading appearance of a wide range of interests. In the end, however, as Nilsen demonstrated, their obsession with themselves makes them tedious to other people. And their narcissism apparently makes it intolerable for them to find themselves pushed to the fringes of other people's mental concern. So even a practising doctor like Harold Shipman found too little ego satisfaction in the life of healing that provides plentiful self-fulfilment for most physicians. Shipman was not, in his own estimation, accorded sufficient respect and admiration by his peers in the medical community. And so, if he couldn't be hailed as the number-one doctor in Hyde, he would play God with his patients, deciding arbitrarily whether this one (whom his colleagues might have allowed a merciful release) should stay alive, while that one (who showed no signs of serious anno domini) should have her life prematurely terminated. Just so does Browning's *Caliban* compensate, by mindless acts of mercy and cruelty, for the nagging sense that he is not really self-sufficient or worth anything:

> 'Am strong myself, compared to yonder crabs
> That march now from the mountain to the sea;
> 'Let twenty pass, and stone the twenty-first,
> Loving not, hating not, just choosing so.

"It's a fact, again, of power control," says Robert Ressler, contemplating Shipman's hunger for "authority over another human being, which, in fact, is what psychopaths get their kicks from...

And taking those lives meant something to him."

In retirement, Ressler's successor, John Douglas, collaborated with the writer Mark Olshaker to explain in books accessible to the general public the remarkable data which he, Ressler and Roy Hazelwood had long been putting before the academic community in learned journals. In the year of Harold Shipman's arrest Douglas and Olshaker's *The Anatomy of Motive* spelled out very clearly the tendency for the apparently "motiveless" murderer to have the real motive of exerting power over others to compensate for feelings of childhood powerlessness and inadequacy he has never outgrown. Thus psychological profiling came to explain the utterly mysterious and pointless conduct of Neill Cream just as an even more puzzling doctor was caught having perpetrated an even larger series of pointless killings.

We are well aware of such people today. A recent book suggests that Alun Kyte may have killed at least 20 women, and that another five or six serial killers are still at large in Britain. While this is almost certainly an overestimate, it is likely enough that no more than three or four individuals were responsible for the dozen or so unsolved "roadside murders" turned up from the files during the investigation into Kyte's murders. But the crime is still extra-ordinarily rare. We are not seriously under threat from "an epidemic" of serial killing. And our means of detection are improving all the time.

DNA identification represents, in Detective Superintendent Kelvin Ashley's view, the biggest step forward for 100 years; an advance comparable with the introduction of fingerprinting. And David Canter and Rupert Heritage proceed apace with the very up-to-date task of turning the fragments of unconscious observation and deduction that make up the traditional "copper's hunch" into numbers that computers can crunch, while the National Crime Faculty, established in 1995, sets out to ensure that all the necessary criminal intelligence collected by all the police forces in the country can be combined and evaluated by compatible computer programs. The press likes to suggest from time to time that the police are demoralized and incompetent. John Duffy's admission that David Mulcahy also participated in his murders has been erroneously portrayed as somehow discrediting David Canter (who never claimed to have reached any high point of expertise in that, his first case, yet who nevertheless lifted Duffy from suspect number 1,500 to the centre spot from which he could be rightly convicted). Paul Britton's retirement is not made more comfortable by his professional association's taking up the charge that he devised an unsuccessful form of pro-active investigation which was castigated by a judge as completely unacceptable enticement and entrapment: a scandal for which Britton and the Met have been treated as culpably responsible, despite the fact that every stage was vetted and monitored by the Home Office and the Director of Public Prosecutions. So it is a happy accident that we may at this point "see ourselves as others see us".

Robert Ressler takes proper pride in having initiated psychological profiling, criminal identification analysis and the successful VICAP (Violent Crimes Apprehension Program) at the FBI. And how does he see Britain's development in these directions? He thinks the British National Crime Faculty "has exceeded the FBI's capabilities. I think the organization is better. I think the way they interact with mental health professionals throughout the country, and the way they keep a hotline going, and the way they keep contact with the police agencies throughout the country, and the actual structure and physical plant of the National Crime Faculty has exceeded that of the FBI's Behavioral Science Unit."

It is a striking tribute to the march of detective competence in the pursuit of those who kill and kill again.

APPENDIX OF KILLERS AND THEIR VICTIMS

Bold type = definite victims of the named murderer
Plain type = probable but unproved victims of the named murderer
Italic type = doubtfully or wrongly ascribed victims of the named murderer

JACK THE RIPPER

"Fairy Fay"	*December 1887*	*Alleged by press: never proven to exist*
Emma Elizabeth Smith	*April 2, 1888*	*Wrongly ascribed*
Martha Tabram	August 6, 1888	Possibly wrongly ascribed
*Mary Ann "Polly" Nichols	**August 31, 1888**	
*Annie Chapman	**September 8, 1888**	
*Elizabeth Stride	**September 30, 1888**	Possibly wrongly ascribed
*Catherine Eddowes	**September 30, 1888**	
Torso found in New Scotland Yard construction site	*October 3, 1888*	*Wrongly ascribed*
*Mary Jane Kelly	**November 9, 1888**	

Rose Mylett aka Eliza Davis	December 20, 1888	*Wrongly ascribed*
"Clay Pipe" Alice McKenzie	July 17, 1889	*Wrongly ascribed*
Torso found in Pinchin Street	September 10, 1889	*Wrongly ascribed*
Frances Coles	February 13, 1891	*Wrongly ascribed*
Elizabeth Jackson	May/June 1891	*Wrongly ascribed*

*The "canonical five" victims confirmed as accepted by the police in Assistant Commissioner Melville Macnaghten's notes and memoirs. Other contemporary police officers, including Assistant Commissioner Robert Anderson, also believed Martha Tabram to be a Ripper victim. Inspector Henry Moore discounted Elizabeth Stride.

DR THOMAS NEILL CREAM

Flora Cream née Brooks	*August 1877*	*Possibly poisoned or lethally aborted*
Kate Gardener	*May 3, 1879*	*Probably lethally aborted*
Mary Anne Faulkner	August 20, 1879	Lethally aborted, but Cream acquitted
Ellen Stack	*December 1879*	*Possibly poisoned*
Daniel Stott	June 11, 1881	
Ellen Donworth	October 13, 1891	
Matilda Clover	October 21, 1891	
Louisa Harvey	October 23, 1891	Escaped attempt
Alice Marsh	April 12, 1892	
Emma Shrivell	April 12, 1892	

Violet Beverley   May 17, 1892   Escaped attempt

GEORGE CHAPMAN (BORN SEVERIN KLOSOWSKI)

Isabella Spink   December 25, 1897
Bessie Taylor   February 13, 1901
Maud Marsh   October 22, 1902

GEORGE JOSEPH SMITH

Bessie Munday   July 13, 1912
Alice Burnham   December 12, 1913
Margaret Lofty   December 18, 1915

GORDON FREDERICK CUMMINS

Margaret Hamilton   February 9, 1942
Evelyn Oatley   February 10, 1942
aka Nita Ward
Margaret Lowe   February 11, 1942
Doris Jouannet   February 14, 1942
Greta Heywood   February 14, 1942   Assaulted but escaped
Cathleen Mulcahy   February 14, 1942   Assaulted but escaped
aka Kate King

JOHN GEORGE HAIGH

William McSwan   September 9, 1944
Young woman from   *February 1945*   *Invented by Haigh*

Hammersmith

Donald McSwan	July 6, 1945	
Amy McSwan	July 6, 1945	
"Max" from	*Autumn 1945*	*Invented by Haigh*
Kensington		
Dr Archie Henderson	February 13, 1948	
Rosalie Henderson	February 13, 1948	
"Mary" from	*Autumn 1948*	*Invented by Haigh*
Eastbourne		
Olive Durand	February 18, 1949	
Deacon		

JOHN REGINALD HALLIDAY CHRISTIE

Ruth Fuerst	August 1943	
Muriel Eady	October 1944	
Beryl Evans	November 8, 1949	Queried by some writers
Jeraldine Evans	November 10/12, 1949	
Ethel Christie	December 14, 1952	
Rita Nelson	January 1953	
Kathleen Maloney	January 1953	
Hectorina MacLennan	March 5, 1953	

PETER MANUEL

Anne Kneilands	January 3, 1956
Marion Watt	September 16, 1956
Margaret Brown	September 16, 1956
Vivienne Brown	September 16, 1956

Stanley Dunn   Early December 1957 Untested in court
Isabelle Cooke   December 28, 1957
Peter Smart   December 31, 1957
Doris Smart   December 31, 1957
Michael Smart   December 31, 1957

"JACK THE STRIPPER": THE "NUDES IN THE THAMES" MURDERER

Elizabeth Figgis   *June 1959*   *Probably wrongly*
                                               connected
Gwynneth Rees   *November 1963*   *Probable abortion*
                                               victim
Hannah Tailford   February 2, 1964
Irene Lockwood   April 8, 1964
Helen Barthelemy   April 24, 1964
Mary Fleming   July 14, 1964
Margaret McGowan   October 23, 1964
Bridie O'Hara   February 16, 1965

IAN BRADY AND MYRA HINDLEY: THE "MOORS MURDERERS"

Pauline Reade   July 12, 1963
John Kilbride   November 23, 1963
Keith Bennett   June 16, 1964
Lesley Ann Downey   December 26, 1964
Edward Evans   October 6, 1965

"BIBLE JOHN"

Patricia Docker	February 22, 1968
Jemima MacDonald	August 1969
Helen Puttock	October 30, 1969

PATRICK MACKAY

Heidi Mnilk	July 1973	Possible but not proved
Mary Hynes	July 1973	
Stephanie Britton	January 12, 1974	Probable but not proved
Christopher Martin	January 12, 1974	Probable but not proved
Unnamed tramp, whose existence is unproved	January 1974	Possible but unlikely
Isabella Griffiths	February 14, 1974	
Frank Goodman	June 1974	
Sarah Rodwell	December 23, 1974	Possible but unlikely
Adele Price	March 10, 1975	
Father Anthony Crean	March 21, 1975	

PETER SUTCLIFFE: THE "YORKSHIRE RIPPER"

Tracey Brown	1975	Survived assault
Anna Rogulskyj	July 5, 1975	Survived savage assault
Olive Smelt	August 15, 1975	Survived savage assault
Wilma McCann	October 30, 1975	

Joan Harrison	November 20, 1975	Claimed by hoaxer
Emily Jackson	January 20, 1976	
Marcella Claxton	May 9, 1976	Survived savage assault
Irene Richardson	February 6, 1977	
Patricia ("Tina") Atkinson	April 23, 1977	
Jayne MacDonald	June 26, 1977	
Maureen Long	July 9, 1977	Survived savage assault
Jean Jordan	October 1, 1977	
Marilyn Moore	December 14, 1977	Survived savage assault
Yvonne Pearson	January 21, 1978	
Helen Rytka	January 31, 1978	
Vera Millward	May 16, 1978	
Josephine Whittaker	April 4, 1979	
Barbara Leach	September 1, 1979	
Marguerite Walls	August 18, 1980	
Dr Upadhya Bandara	October 1980	Survived savage assault
Theresa Sykes	November 5, 1980	Survived assault
Jacqueline Hill	November 17, 1980	

DENNIS NILSEN

Unknown Irishman	January 1, 1979	
Andrew Ho	August 1979	Survived assault
Kenneth Ockenden	December 3, 1979	
Martyn Duffey	May 17, 1980	
Billy Sutherland	July 7, 1980	
Unknown half-Latino	September/October 1980	
Douglas Stewart	November 12, 1980	Survived assault
Unknown Willesden Irishman	c. November 1980	

Unknown emaciated man	December 1980	
Unknown hippie	late December 1980	
Unknown Scotsman	early 1981	
Unknown young man	spring 1981	
Unknown skinhead	summer 1981	
Malcolm Barlow	August 18, 1981	
Paul Nobbs	November 25, 1981	Survived assault
John Peter Howlett	March 1982	
Carl Stotter aka Kharla Le Fox	May 1982	Survived assault
Graham Allan	late 1982	
Toshimitsu Ozawa	December 31, 1982	Survived assault
Stephen Sinclair	January 26, 1983	

JOHN DUFFY AND DAVID MULCAHY

Alison Day	January 15, 1986	
Maartje Tamboezer	April 17, 1986	
Anne Lock	May 18, 1986	

MICHELE DE MARCO LUPO

James Burns	March 15, 1986	
James Connolly	April 3, 1986	
Unnamed tramp	April 18, 1986	
Mark Leyland	April 18, 1986	Assaulted but escaped
Damien McLuskey	April 1986	

David Cole	May 1986	Assaulted but escaped

KENNETH ERSKINE

Eileen Emms	April 9, 1986	
Jane Cockett	June 1986	
Valentine Gleim	June 1986	
Zbigniew Strabawa	June 1986	
Fred Prentice	June 27, 1986	Assaulted but escaped
William Carmen	July 1986	
William Downes	July 1986	
Florence Tisdall	July 1986	

FRED AND ROSEMARY WEST

Robin Holt	March 1, 1967	Apparent suicide: Fred possibly involved
Annie McFall	August 1967	Fred solo
Mary Bastholm	January 6, 1968	Probably Fred solo
Charmaine West	June 1971	Probably Rose solo
Catherine ("Rena") West	August 1971	Probably Fred solo
Lynda Gough	April 19, 1973	
Carol Ann Cooper	November 10, 1973	
Lucy Partington	December 27, 1973	
Thérèse Siegenthaler	April 16, 1974	
Shirley Hubbard	November 14, 1974	
Juanita Mott	April 11, 1975	

Shirley Robinson	June 1978
Alison Chambers	September 1979
Heather West	June 19, 1987

ROBERT BLACK

April Fabb	April 8, 1969	Highly probable but unproven
Christine Markham	1973	Possible but unproven
Genette Tate	August 19, 1978	Highly probable but unproven
Suzanne Lawrence	1979	Possible but unproven
Susan Maxwell	July 30, 1982	
Caroline Hogg	July 8, 1983	
Sarah Harper	March 26, 1986	
Teresa Thornhill	April 28, 1988	Probable but rescued
Patsy Morris	1990	Possible but unproven
Mandy Wilson	July 14, 1990	Assaulted but rescued
Marion Crofts		Possible but unproven
Lisa Hession		Possible but unproven

COLIN IRELAND

| Peter Walker | March 8, 1993 |

Christopher Dunn	May 28, 1993	
Perry Bradley III	June 4, 1993	
Andrew Collier	June 7, 1993	
Emanuel Spiteri	June 12, 1993	

PETER MOORE

Henry Roberts	September 1995
Edward Carthy	October 1995
Keith Randles	November 1995
Tony Davies	December 1995

DR HAROLD SHIPMAN

Mary Winterbottom	1984	Suspected
Eileen Cox	September 21, 1984	Suspected
May Brookes	February 14, 1985	Suspected
Margaret Conway	February 1985	Suspected
Nancy Brassington	September 14, 1987	Suspected
Monica Sparkes	October 7, 1987	Suspected
John Charlton	October 16, 1987	Suspected
Alice Prestwich	October 20, 1987	Suspected
Hilda Couzens	February 24, 1993	Suspected
Olive Heginbotham	February 25, 1993	Suspected
Amy Whitehead	March 22, 1993	Suspected
Sarah Ashworth	April 17, 1993	Inquest verdict
Nellie Mullen	May 2, 1993	Suspected
Edna Llewellyn	May 4, 1993	Suspected
Emily Morgan	May 12, 1993	Suspected
Violet Bird	May 13, 1993	Suspected

Joan Harding	January 4, 1994	Suspected
Christine Hancock	January 13, 1994	Suspected
Elsie Platt	February 9, 1994	Suspected
Mary Smith	May 17, 1994	Suspected
Alice Kitchen	June 17, 1994	Inquest verdict
Maria Thornton	July 28, 1994	Suspected
Lizzie Mellor	November 20, 1994	Suspected
John Molesdale	December 29, 1994	Suspected
Alice Kennedy	January 9, 1995	Suspected
Lucy Virgin	March 1, 1995	Suspected
Marie West	March 6, 1995	
Netta Ashcroft	March 7, 1995	Suspected
Marie Fernley	March 13, 1995	Suspected
Edith Scott	April 13, 1995	Suspected
Renata Overton	April 21, 1995	Suspected
Violet Bird	May 13, 1995	Suspected
Bertha Moss	June 13, 1995	Suspected
Ada Hilton	July 12, 1995	Suspected
Geoffrey Bogle	September 14, 1995	Suspected
Dora Ashton	September 26, 1995	Suspected
Muriel Ward	October 24, 1995	Suspected
Edith Brock	November 8, 1995	Suspected
Hilda Hibbert	January 2, 1996	Suspected
Erla Copeland	January 11, 1996	Suspected
Jane Shelmerdine	February 21, 1996	Suspected
Marjorie Waller	April 18, 1996	Suspected
Elsie Godfrey	May 7, 1996	Suspected
Edith Brady	May 13, 1996	Suspected
Valerie Cuthbert	May 29, 1996	Suspected
Lillian Cullen	May 30, 1996	Suspected
Gladys Saunders	June 17, 1996	Suspected
Carrie Leigh	June 22, 1996	Suspected

Marion Higham	June 25, 1996	Suspected
Elsie Hannible	June 30, 1996	Suspected
Irene Turner	July 11, 1996	
Sidney Smith	August 30, 1996	Suspected
Dorothy Andrew	September 12, 1996	Suspected
Annie Ralphs	September 20, 1996	Suspected
Millicent Garside	October 22, 1996	Suspected
Irene Heathcote	November 20, 1996	Suspected
Conrad Robinson	November 25, 1996	Suspected
Thomas Cheetham	December 4, 1996	Suspected
Ken Smith	December 17, 1996	Suspected
Elsie Dean	January 8, 1997	Suspected
Irene Brooder	January 20, 1997	Suspected
Lottie Bennison	January 27, 1997	Suspected
Joyce Woodhead	February 23, 1997	Suspected
Lizzie Adams	February 28, 1997	
Rose Garlick	March 22, 1997	Suspected
May Lowe	March 27, 1997	Suspected
Mary Coutts	April 21, 1997	Suspected
Elsie Cheetham	April 25, 1997	Suspected
Jean Lilley	April 25, 1997	
Lena Slater	May 2, 1997	Suspected
Ethel Kellett	May 13, 1997	Suspected
Doris Earls	May 21, 1997	Suspected
Ivy Lomas	May 29, 1997	
Muriel Grimshaw	July 14, 1997	
Lily Newby	July 28, 1997	Suspected
Nancy Jackson	September 1, 1997	Suspected
Mavis Pickup	September 22, 1997	Suspected
Bessie Swann	September 27, 1997	Suspected
Enid Otter	September 29, 1997	Suspected
Florence Lewis	November 10, 1997	Suspected

Bertha Parr	November 11, 1997	Suspected
Mary Walls	November 14, 1997	Suspected
Elizabeth Baddeley	November 21, 1997	Suspected
Marie Quinn	November 24, 1997	
Elizabeth Battersby	December 8, 1997	Suspected
Kathleen Wagstaff	December 9, 1997	
Bianka Pomfret	December 10, 1997	
Alice Black	December 18, 1997	Suspected
James King	December 24, 1997	Suspected
Mabel Shawcross	January 22, 1997	Suspected
Norah Nuttall	January 26, 1998	
Cissie Davis	February 3, 1998	Suspected
Pamela Hillier	February 9, 1998	
Laura Linn	February 13 1998	Suspected
Irene Berry	February 15, 1998	Suspected
Maureen Ward	February 18, 1998	
Joan Dean	February 27, 1998	Suspected
Harold Eddleston	March 4, 1998	Suspected
Margaret Waldron	March 6, 1998	Suspected
Irene Chapman	March 7, 1998	Suspected
Lily Higgins	March 17, 1998	Suspected
Ada Warburton	May 11, 1998	Suspected
Winifred Mellor	May 11, 1998	
Joan Melia	June 12, 1998	
Kathleen Grundy	June 24, 1998	

The above cases merited police investigation. In addition, Dr Richard Baker's official audit of Shipman's records postulated that he might have been killing patients from almost the beginning of his career, and his total number of victims could possibly exceed 300.

ALUN KYTE

Yvonne Coley	1984	Possible connection
Gail Whitehouse	October 1990	Possible connection
Janine Downes	February 1991	Possible connection
Diane McInally	1991	Possible connection
Barbara Finn	1991	Possible connection
Nicola Payne	1991	Possible connection
Lynne Trenholme	June 1991	Possible connection
Natalie Pearman	November 1992	Possible connection
Mandy Duncan	1993	Possible connection
Carol Clark	March 1993	Possible connection
Samo Paull	December 1993	
Tracy Turner	March 3, 1994	
Dawn Shields	May 21, 1994	Possible connection
Emma Merry	May 1994	Possible connection
Sharon Harper	July 1994	Possible connection
Jane Clayton	July 1994	Possible connection
Julie Finlay	August 1994	Possible connection
Mary Garrity	1995	Possible connection
Céline Figard	January 1996	

BIBLIOGRAPHY

Anderson, Sir Robert, *Criminals and Crime*, Nisbet, London, 1907
— *The Lighter Side of My Official Life*, Hodder & Stoughton, London, 1910
Beadle, William, *Jack the Ripper: Anatomy of a Myth*, Wat Tyler, Dagenham, 1995
Begg, Paul, *Jack the Ripper: The Uncensored Facts*, Robson, London, 1988
— with Martin Fido and Keith Skinner, *The Jack the Ripper A to Z*, Headline, London, 1991
— with Keith Skinner, *The Scotland Yard Files*, Headline, London, 1992
Briffett, David, *The Acid Bath Murders*, Briffett, Horsham, 1997
Britton, Paul, *The Jigsaw Man*, Corgi, London, 1998
Browne, Douglas G., and Tullett E.V., *Bernard Spilsbury*, Harrap, London, 1952
Burn, Gordon, *Somebody's Husband, Somebody's Son*, Pan, London, 1985
Camps, Francis, *Medical and Scientific Investigations in the Christie Case*, Medical Publications, London, 1953

Canter, David, *Criminal Shadows*, HarperCollins, London, 1995

Caputi, Jane, *The Age of Sex Crime*, Women's Press, London, 1987

Clark, Steve, with Morley, Mike, *Murder in Mind: Mindhunting the Serial Killers*, Boxtree, London, 1993

Clark, Tim, with Penycate, John, *Psychopath*, Routledge & Kegan Paul, London, 1976

Connell, Nicholas, with Evans, Stewart P., *The Man Who Hunted Jack the Ripper: Edmund Reid and the Police Perspective*, Rupert Books, Cambridge, 1999

Conradi, Peter, *The Red Ripper*, True Crime, London, 1992

Cross, Roger, *The Yorkshire Ripper*, Grafton, London, 1981

Cullen, Tom, *Autumn of Terror*, Bodley Head, London, 1965

Dew, Walter, *I Caught Crippen*, Blackie, Edinburgh, 1938

Douglas, John, with Olshaker, Mark, *Mindhunter*, Scribner, New York, 1995

— *The Anatomy of Motive*, Scribner, New York, 1999

—*The Cases That Haunt Us: From Jack the Ripper to JonBenét Ramsey*, Scribner, New York, 2000

Du Rose, John, *Murder Was My Business*, Mayflower, London, 1973

Dvorchak, Robert J., with Holewa, Lisa, *Milwaukee Massacre*, Dell, New York, 1991

Eddowes, John, *The Two Killers of Rillington Place*, Little, Brown, London, 1994

Eddowes, Michael, *The Man on Your Conscience*, Cassell, London, 1955

Evans, Stewart P.

— with Gainey, Paul, *The Lodger: The Arrest and Escape of Jack the Ripper*, Century, London, 1995

— with Skinner, Keith, *The Ultimate Jack the Ripper Source Book*, Robson, London, 2000

Farson, Daniel, *Jack the Ripper*, Michael Joseph, London, 1972

Fido, Martin, *The Crimes, Detection and Death of Jack the Ripper,*

Orion, London, 1993

— *The Chronicle of Crime*, Carlton Books, London, 2000

— with Skinner, Keith, *The Official Encyclopedia of Scotland Yard*, Virgin, London, 2000

Firmin, Stanley, *Crime Man*, Hutchinson, London, 1950

Gekoski, Anna, *Murder by Numbers: British Serial Killers Since 1950*, André Deutsch, London, 1999

Gibney, Bruce, *The Beauty Queen Killer*, Pinnacle, New York, 1990

Hansford Johnson, Pamela, *On Iniquity*, Macmillan, London, 1967

Harrison, Shirley, *The Diary of Jack the Ripper*, Smith Gryphon, London, 1993

Jackson, Robert, *Francis Camps*, Hart-Davis, London, 1975

Jesse, F. Tennyson (ed.) *Trials of Timothy John Evans and John Reginald Halliday Christie*, William Hodge, Edinburgh, 1957

Kelleher, Michael D., and C.L., *Murder Most Rare: The Female Serial Killer*, Dell, New York, 1998

Kennedy, Ludovic, *10 Rillington Place*, Gollancz, London, 1961

Keppel, Robert D., with Birnes, William J., *Signature Killers*, Arrow, London, 1998

Keyes, Edward, *The Michigan Murders*, New English Library, London, 1977

LaBern, Arthur, Haigh, *The Mind of a Murderer*, W.H. Allen, London, 1973

Lefebure, Molly, *Evidence for the Crown*, Ace, London, 1957

Leyton, Elliott, *Hunting Humans*, Penguin, Harmondsworth, 1989

Lucas, Norman, *The Sex Killers*, True Crime, London, 1992

Linedecker, Clifford L., *Thrill Killers*, Futura, London, 1990

McConnell, Brian, *Found Naked and Dead*, New English Library, London, 1974

— with Bence, Douglas, *The Nilsen File*, Futura, London, 1983

Macnaghten, Sir Melville L., *Days of My Years*, Edward Arnold, London, 1914

Marjoribanks, Edward, *Famous Trials of Marshall Hall*, Penguin, Harmondsworth, 1989

Marriner, Brian, *Forensic Clues to Murder*, Arrow, London, 1991

— *A Century of Sex Killers*, True Crime, London, 1992

Masters, Brian, *Killing for Company*, Jonathan Cape, London, 1985

Mendoza, Antonio, *Killers on the Loose*, Virgin, London, 2000

Molloy, Pat, *The Cannock Chase Murders*, New English Library, 1990

Morton, James, *The Who's Who of Unsolved Murders*, Kyle Cathie, London, 1995

Nash, Jay Robert, *World Encyclopedia of 20th Century Murder*, Headline, London, 1992

Norris, Joel, *Serial Killers: The Growing Menace*, Arrow, London, 1998

O'Gara, Noel, *The Real Yorkshire Ripper Revealed*, O'Gara, Athlone, 1989

Paget, R.T., with Silverman, Sydney, *Hanged – and Innocent?* Gollancz, London, 1953

Paley, Bruce, *Jack the Ripper: The Simple Truth*, Headline, London, 1995

Paul, Philip, *Murder Under the Microscope*, Futura, London, 1990

Phillips, Conrad, *Murderers' Moon*, Arthur Barker, London, 1956

Ressler, Robert K., with Shachtman, Tom, *Whoever Fights Monsters*, St Martin's, New York, 1992

Ritchie, Jean, *150 Years of True Crime Stories*, O'Mara Books, London, 1993

— *Myra Hindley*, Angus & Robertson, London, 1988

Rumbelow, Donald, *The Complete Jack the Ripper*, Penguin, Harmondsworth, 1987

Sanders, John, *Forensic Casebook of Crime*, True Crime, London, 2000

Simpson, Keith, *Forty Years of Murder*, Harrap, London, 1978

Sounes, Howard, *Fred and Rose*, Warner, London, 1995

Stalker, John, *Stalker*, Harrap, London, 1988

Stern, Chester, *Dr Iain West's Casebook*, Warner, London, 1997

Topping, Peter, with Ritchie, Jean, *Topping*, Angus & Robertson, London, 1989

Wansell, Geoffrey, *An Evil Love: The Life of Frederick West*, Headline, London, 1997

West, Ann, *For the Love of Lesley*, W.H. Allen, London, 1989

West, Stephen, and Mae, *Inside 25 Cromwell St*, Peter Grose, Monmouth, 1995

Whittington-Egan, Richard, *A Casebook on Jack the Ripper*, Wiley, London, 1975

Williams, Emlyn, *Beyond Belief*, Random House, New York, 1968

Wilson, Colin, *Written in Blood*, HarperCollins, Glasgow, 1995

Yallop, David, *Deliver Us From Evil*, Futura, London, 1981

INDEX

PICTURE CREDITS